Vern-Lois
To

TO Christopher

from

Dennis + Eva

TAKEN AT

GUNPOINT

...in the Andes

by Tina Knight

Trust you enjoy it!

Blessings as you read!

Tina Knight

John 15:16

WinePress Publishing Mukilteo, WA 98275

From
Grandma Ellis

DEDICATED

to our children
Gary, Beverly, and Karen,
who made our work a happy and
satisifying experience.

TABLE OF CONTENTS

INTRODUCTION

"The Aymaras pled for a Bible Training School. They want to be pastors but need someone to teach them." In the early months of 1945 we sat in the Friends church at Greenleaf, Idaho, listening to Walter Lee, mission board president, report on his recent trip to Bolivia.

Walter's challenge gripped our hearts that cold winter night. Roscoe squeezed my arm and whispered, "That's for us." We promptly responded to the plea from Bolivia.

I've written the story of Copajira, the mission farm, the Helen Cammack Memorial Bible Training School, and their contribution to the development of the Bolivian Friends Church. As I write human interest stories, I trust young people will feel the challenge of missions and answer God's call to the greatest service they can render their Lord. I'm also hoping to challenge others to prayer and the support of missions.

At first I thought to write the story without involving the Knight family but I could not. We take no praise for what God has done but are thankful for the privilege of being a part of it, and of working with co-workers who could also add their stories. Seven fellow-workers have gone on to Heaven, giving me a sense of urgency to publish the story. It does not refer directly or indirectly to the Roman Catholic religion except as it exists in Latin America.

Most of the data has been gleaned from letters kept by our parents for forty years, but I've also included bits and pieces from periodicals and other published works: <u>Soul Cry of the Aymara</u>, <u>Northwest Friend</u>, <u>The Missionary Voice of Evangelical Friends</u>, <u>Bolivian Friends from Mission to Yearly Meeting</u>, <u>From One to Multiplication, and Missionary Moments</u>.

These years have witnessed the fulfillment of God's promise that His Word would not return unto Him void and "he that goeth forth and weepeth, bearing precious seed, shall doubtless come again with rejoicing, bringing his sheaves with him." (Psalm126:6)

Tina Knight, February 1996

PROLOGUE

Delirious, he tossed on a bed of dingy homespun blankets. Foul air of a dark room pressed in upon him. His fever climbed higher but no one wet his parched lips with a sip of cool water nor sponged his fevered brow. Others in the room discussed this foreigner in a guttural language he could not understand.

"Who was this foreigner?" they asked. In Bolivia only a handful knew him. But God knew him as a faithful servant who had "fought a good fight, finished the course, and kept the faith." Gasping for air, he died alone in the General Hospital in La Paz, Bolivia, in 1919.

William Able was born on the San Pasqual Indian Reservation, in southern California, the son of a Dutch Jewish father and American Indian mother. Left an orphan at an early age, he passed from family to family, and finally finished the seventh grade at 23 years of age. Later he became a butcher and spent his wages on gambling and drink.

Acknowledging the emptiness of his life, William accepted the Lord Jesus as Savior in a Friends church in southern California. He studied in a Bible Training School, then spent 11 years in missionary work in the Philippines. After recovering from a bout with malaria in the States, he answered God's call for colportage work, selling Scriptures, in Bolivia.

A freighter trip along the west coast of South America dropped William off at Mollendo, Peru, where he boarded a train and rode a narrow-gauge railway through crescent dunes in the desert. Climbing over the Andes, he passed herds of vicuña, alpaca, and the haughty, aristocratic llama. At night he crossed Lake Titicaca on a steamship that had been carried over the Andes piece by piece on the backs of animals and assembled on the shores of this 12,500-foot-high lake.

On the train again, as he passed the ruins of Tiahuanaco, the cradle of Aymara civilization, he wondered about these people who lived in adobe homes splashed with blood and topped with straw crosses on thatched roofs. Oxen, adorned with flags, plowed in postage-stamp-size fields; men, women, and children, hardy folk, trotted rocky paths barefooted or in sandals but seemingly bundled in layers of woolens to ward off the cold wind whipping down from the snow-covered Cordillera to the north.

William Able didn't know that the roots of these indomitable people reached back 250 years before the time of Christ. The Incas conquered the Aymara kingdom in 1452. Later the Spanish took control but the Aymaras were never subjugated by their conquerors. They clung tenaciously to their animistic culture and guttural language. Slaves to the Spanish serf system, they became heirs of oppression and hatred. To these people William had come to bring the Gospel of Jesus Christ.

Triple peaks of Mt. Illimani towered over La Paz, a city of 100,000 people pressed into the canyon, or "kettle" as they called it. A stranger, with no friends nor family, William settled in as one more in the mass of humanity. He struggled with the high altitude, which affected his heart. Undaunted, however, wrapped in his fur-collared overcoat, he took his guitar out into the street to sing and preach.

Eight months later William Able succumbed to smallpox but not before casting his mantle, along with his guitar, upon the shoulders of one of his first converts, grandson of a Roman Catholic priest, a young mestizo, Juan Ayllón.

The seed William Able planted has continued to produce a harvest of Aymara souls throughout the years. In 1930 the first American missionaries from Oregon Yearly Meeting of Friends Church, now Northwest Yearly Meeting, arrived in La Paz, accepting the challenge of missionary work started by Juan Ayllón. During the time period covered in this book we joined 14 couples and two single women who contributed to that harvest.

1

BOLIVIA

Giant boulders reached out to grab the wings of our DC-3 as it labored up the steep Andean canyon. Leaving the coastal fog behind we climbed to dizzying heights, but never far above thatch-roofed adobe huts and postage-stamp-size fields. The snow-capped Andean Cordillera cast it's shadow into the deep blue waters of Lake Titicaca, the highest navigable lake in the world. With little time to exclaim over the beauty, we circled the bowl in which La Paz is built and set down on the highest commercial airport in the world. A brown and white llama grazed beneath a sign that read, "La Paz, Bolivia, 4,062 metros (13,404 feet)." After 47 hours of flying time we landed October 29, 1945, with excitement and wonder. *What did God have for us, two 23 year old missionaries, in this land of superlatives?*

From the rim of the bowl we looked down on a city of one-story adobe houses with red tile roofs. Our five senses immediately exploded as we wound our way around the sides of the bowl down into town for a closer look. Sights, sounds, smells, taste, and even touch opened a whole new way of life for us.

People crowded the steep, cobblestone streets of the city. Aymara women in many bright homespun skirts, shawls, and derby hats carried babies on their backs; Aymara men clad in homespun trousers, ponchos, and *abarcas* (sandals made of rubber tires), wore hats atop knit *gorros* pulled low over their brows.

These *mamas* and *tatas* either milled the streets, looking for a bargain, or sat behind piles of oranges, onions, potatoes, jerky, and *ají*, red chili pods. Some were almost hidden by huge cloth bags of *coca* leaves. Others sold candles, vegetable dyes, giant safety pins, and nails. Crowded close by, a toothless *tata* offered a dozen or so empty bottles for sale. On a side street vendors set up tables displaying witchcraft paraphernalia—llama fetuses, starfish, herbs, and incense. It seemed everyone had something to sell.

Bolivia intrigued us. Every day we learned something new. Lack of sanitation in most Aymara homes and open sewers aroused our sense of smell whenever we left the house. But the smell of a clay pot of soup simmering over a clay stove in some believer's kitchen whet our appetites for that delicious Bolivian staple, mutton or guinea pig soup with *chuños*, dehydrated potatoes, onion, and *ají*.

Beggars wandered through the crowds whining for a coin. Some sat at the entrance of large churches, taking advantage of the belief that giving alms earned favor with God. Still others, blind or crippled, were strategically placed as professional beggars.

Sights and sounds mingled as rickety buses, horns honking, slowly wound their way through the crowds. Ancient streetcars, hanging low at both ends, rattled up the steep narrow-gauge lines.

Aymaras celebrated fiestas with alcohol and danced to the music of drum, charango (stringed instrument made from the armadillo), and bamboo flutes, *quena* and *sampoña (panpipe)*. "Aye, aye, aye-aye." A nasal song echoed across the crisp night air as an inebriated celebrant staggered home from the fiesta. Sometimes an equally soused buddy shared this euphoric struggle over cobblestone streets. Other times a faithful companion waited, shivering in the cold, to guide her husband home.

Ding, dong—dong, dong, dong—ding, ding, dong. The bells from Gran Poder church nearby, a rooster's crow, the donkey's mournful bray, and the blaring horn of an impatient truck driver echoed through the streets announcing the beginning of a new day in La Paz, Bolivia.

La Paz...where in 1919, William Able, a native American Indian arrived to preach the Gospel.

...where William left his guitar with one convert, Juan Ayllón, then went on to Heaven as a result of smallpox.

...where that one Aymara believer grew to many Aymara converts who welcomed the missionaries—Tamplin, Pearson, Cammack, Gulley, and Chapman.

...where 26 years after William Able arrived, the church welcomed the Knights with baskets of flowers and *abrazos*, hugs.

As some 300 earth-toned Aymara believers welcomed us with baskets of kantutas, Bolivian national flower, we remembered again God's call in Greenleaf, Idaho. We felt anew the challenge of older men clothed in homespun as they pled for a school. Younger ones, longing for schooling beyond the third grade, added to the plea. Even *señoritas*, lifting their striped shawls to partially cover their faces, then lowering their eyes so as not to appear bold, silently pled for a school. They longed for a school where girls could achieve more than the normal home education of learning to cook mutton or *chuño* soup or how to spin yarn and weave cloth.

As we embraced long lines of believers, God confirmed our call to the Aymara.

La Paz, Bolivia

Street Market

Knight's welcome to Bolivia, 1945.

2

FORTY-FIVE BULLET HOLES

Upon our arrival in Bolivia we endeavored to learn the Spanish language, to become acquainted with the Aymara people, to be involved in the mission work, and to learn customs of the country. We soon discovered some strange but important regulations necessary for living in a foreign country.

It is impossible to live in Bolivia any length of time without legal papers. So the first order of business required that we obtain our personal identification cards. Howard Pearson, fellow missionary, accompanied us to town to start this process the day after we arrived. After being in Bolivia two terms, he had forgotten that newcomers were very short of breath in the extreme altitude. Probably he had also forgotten that most missionaries didn't have legs as long as his. We panted to keep up and wondered, "What's the hurry?"

To secure ID cards necessitated umpteen visits to umpteen offices; purchasing sheets of legal paper and official stamps; having all fingers and thumbs pressed into an ink pad, then carefully rolled across official paper; and after futilely trying to wipe the ink off on a filthy rag, being told, "Come back tomorrow." Of course we went back, only to hear again, "Come back tomorrow." It was frustrating but one can't live in Bolivia without going through the process. We learned patience when visiting government offices in Bolivia.

Shortly after arriving in Bolivia Roscoe applied for a driver's license. The long process covered several weeks, required visiting nine government offices and taking a test involving tricky parking and one-way streets.

Here are Roscoe's seven steps to a driver's license:
1. Buy a sheet of official stationery at one office.
2. Walk one block to our lawyer's office to have him write a petition to the Chief of Police for a good conduct certificate.
3. Take certificate two blocks to the police station, buy a stamp for the paper, take it to two offices, give them my life history, then wait a half hour for the certificate.
4. Get a health certificate from an eye doctor.
5. Take all these documents to the *Tránsito*, traffic department. Take a stiff driver's test: tell which streets are one-way and which way (they aren't always marked); back your vehicle down a steep, narrow, crooked street; run your fender under the bed of a truck, etc.
6. Finally I'm granted a provisional license for a few months.

7. Take another test and at last get a permanent license!

After obtaining our ID cards from Immigration and Roscoe's provisional driver's license, we moved to an apartment of our own. We had lived at the mission house with Ralph and Marie Chapman and three-year-old Linnea for two months, a time that provided a necessary learning experience for living in another culture. Our new home across town from the mission, a five-room apartment costing $45 a month, was also across the street from the arsenal.

Next, we settled into language study. Three times a week *Señor* Rada, a Spanish teacher, came to our apartment to tutor us. Within three months Roscoe began leading services. After another couple of months, he started preaching in Spanish. Obviously, he was a linguist. As for me, I struggled.

In order to become better acquainted with the field during our first year, we visited all the churches and took two trips over the Andes that required a bit of stamina; one to Mina Fabulosa and the other to Chusi.

Uma Palca Friends Church was located just below the richest tin mine in the world, Mina Fabulosa, at 15,000 feet above sea level in the Andean range. Missionary men made the trip on foot, but I rode a mule 12 miles from the end of the road. Aside from my being a bit sore and the fright I felt when the sharp switchbacks left my mule's hindquarters hanging out over an abyss below, it was a "fun" trip.

It was also a beautiful trip. We climbed up, up, up over a snow-covered trail, then across a glacier, being careful to stay close to the trail for fear of falling into enormous crevasses where rainbows of colors painted exquisite patterns. Under the lee of a dark blue ice cavern one could seek shelter from storms if needed. Both beauty and altitude were breathtaking!

Two hours later we crossed the pass then followed a trail down the valley. Aymara believers, a part of our church family, greeted us at their little adobe and rock church nestled among the boulders. "*Mamas*" were especially excited that a woman missionary had come to visit them. The trip resulted in a spiritual feast for everyone.

The trip to Chusi, a colonization project organized by the National Holiness Missionary Society (World Gospel Mission), also proved exciting. Chusi, located on the eastern slopes of the Andes mountains in an area of narrow ravines, sheer cliffs, and raging rivers, could only be reached by swinging footbridges, and stair-step rock trails. Rock outcroppings on these narrow trails sometimes caught the loads of pack animals, sending them over the precipice. It was an inaccessible area for anything other than man and beast.

Seven missionaries, Oather and Ruth Perkinson, Homer and Elvira Firestone, Marshal Cavit, and Roscoe and I, packed into a Jeep, then labored up Mt. Iliampu to the end of the road. From there, we womenfolk rode mules while the men walked for three days.

The first night, bedded down between boulders out under the stars, we shivered in our sleeping bags on an icy Andean pass. The second night we arrived at a rock hut just before sundown.

"I'd be glad to have you stay, but..." Our host hesitated when we asked for lodging, then added, "Sure, it will be ready in a minute."

He ran the pigs out of a low hut. With a short wiry grass broom, he swept the floor, covered it with straw, then said, "Welcome."

We couldn't question the shelter that he offered. After all, we had ridden a mule or walked all day. The icy wind from glaciers above whipped down upon us at 11,000 feet. Stiff, hungry, and tired, we weren't concerned with the condition of the accommodations.

Marshal hastily opened his cans of sardines; we prepared to eat supper. Alas, those sardines proved to be squid. Ugh! But squid is better than nothing if eaten with a cracker and washed down with a hot drink. We soon felt satisfied and crawled into our sleeping bags.

Sometime in the middle of the night it started to rain. Marshal picked up his sleeping bag and left, then we noted water flowing through the lower side of our hut. We six pulled up our feet and slept curled until morning. After all, it was raining, miserable, cold, and there was no place to go so why get up?

Marshal had taken his bed out to an adobe bench under the eaves of the hut. Rain splattered him a bit but not nearly so much as the chickens that roosted above. We had spent the second night of the trip in a pigpen.

On down the trail next day brought us to Chusi where we shared the hospitality of fellow missionaries and dined on parrot and palm-heart salad. We had experienced the thrill of climbing high rock stairs cut out of the mountain, of crossing heart-stopping swinging bridges, and of traveling from snow-covered Mt. Iliampu to steamy hot jungles. Although transportation and living accommodations weren't the best, the trip to Chusi proved to be an unforgettable Andean adventure.

Soon after arriving in Bolivia Roscoe became Secretary of Education for the mission. He directed four primary schools, a task requiring miles of travel to start classes, deliver supplies, give immunizations, and administer exams. His work with the primary schools, plus being director and teaching night classes in the Bible School at the La Paz church, prepared him for more responsibility in a future Bible School. It also introduced us to our first Bolivian revolution.

La Paz, the capital of Bolivia, does not live up to its name. La Paz means "City of Peace," but the city averaged three revolutions a year. Over the years politics, poverty, lack of transportation, graft and corruption in the government, all caused dissatisfaction, which exploded into revolutions. The lack of paved roads beyond a few in the center of town, stifled commerce. Many a burro bearing either produce from the fields or ore from the mines, picked its way over rocky paths to market in the city. Prices soared. Long lines waited for bread, gas, and other scarce items. Farmers sold their produce for a pittance. Miners slaved for low wages. Exports dwindled to nothing when miners in tungsten, silver, gold, and tin mines went on strike. The labor union, led by *Señor* Lechín, kept the pot of dissatisfaction boiling. A peaceful settlement for all the problems seemed impossible.

Bolivia's reputation for revolutions became reality for me early one morning when I awakened to machine gun rat-a-tat-tat. Someone pounded on my door. Since Roscoe was visiting schools that week, Samuel Smith and son, S.J., missionaries living close by, had come to take me to their home, a safer place than our house across the street from the arsenal. First, they had to convince the soldier stationed outside my door that a lone woman lived inside our apartment.

That revolution sputtered, with no casualties. The next one, a few weeks later, changed the course of history.

After a trip to the country in June 1946, we returned to La Paz to find a revolution in full swing. Cannon fire boomed down into the city from the rim of the Alto above. The road down into town closed so we spent the night dozing on benches at the airport.

Next morning we crept down into town over six inches of new snow. Nearing the cemetery, we met Ralph, who had started out on foot to search for us. Hearing sniper fire we hurriedly turned up back roads, trying to find our way home.

"Get the car off the street," a woman yelled from her doorway. "They're burning cars." Fear and panic clutched us, for no doorway appeared wide enough for a car in that area.

I raised my hands, palms up, showing we were helpless. She braved the narrow, cobblestone alley to give us some much-needed advice. "Put up a white flag." Seeing the tea towel I had over the lunch basket, she snatched it up, commanding, "Use that!"

With a white tea towel flying, we raced through cross fire at the corner, recognized where we were and rounded the corner with horn blaring. Martín, the mission gate keeper recognized the horn (it had the only distinctive sound in town), opened the gate, and we shot into our driveway. Tension was too much; I burst into tears.

We stayed at the mission house three days. Snipers fired from a shield of sandbags near our front gate. Air force planes dropped bombs on strategic areas. Rifle fire echoed across the city day and night. Church services had barely started on Sunday when fighting became more intense so believers ran for home.

When all seemed calm, Ralph and Roscoe started across town to see if everything was all right at our apartment. They hadn't gone far when they met a truck loaded with men bristling with guns. Some hollered at the fellows but they didn't understand them. Several started pantomiming the removal of ties. The men caught on and quickly yanked off their ties. This revolution put the blue-collar worker in power, marking the demise of some of the last trappings of colonialism. That ended the era of the men having to wear ties and jackets every time they stepped out into the street.

Arriving at our house, Roscoe and Ralph found that two bullets had penetrated our walls. One was imbedded in the wall just three inches above our pillows. The other came through a window frame, passed through some song books and the lid of a folding organ, through the hall wall, up through a library tabletop to land in a flowerpot. On the outside of our house, on the side toward the arsenal, the men counted 45 bullet holes.

After spending three days at the mission house, we moved back to our apartment, thinking all was safe. That evening, we started to walk to the post office, not realizing that planes didn't land in La Paz during a revolution and there would be no mail. Arriving at Plaza Murillo, we found it full of people staring in silence at three ministers of government hanging on lampposts in front of the President's palace. President Villaroel had been hung on one of these posts two days earlier.

Hurrying toward home, we mentally listed three good lessons learned about revolutions in Latin America: Revolutions are usually a surprise; revolutions aren't always over when the shooting stops; for safety, don't live across the street from the arsenal.

Aymara Fiesta

Flute Band

3

COPAJIRA

Our goal in going to Bolivia was to start a Bible Training School to prepare Aymara young men and women to serve as pastors and workers in the Friends church. Between Spanish language lessons, visiting churches, trips over the mountains, and revolutions, we, Ralph and Marie Chapman and Roscoe and Tina Knight, sandwiched in several trips to the *altiplano*, high plains, in search of a suitable farm for such a school.

We didn't want a large farm, but one that would provide support for students. We planned for them to study in the mornings and work on the farm in the afternoons for their room and board. Hacienda Copajira impressed us, but the size overwhelmed us: 3,000 acres, with 540 sheep, two ponies, nine cows, six hogs, 15 ducks and a few guinea pigs. Could we handle such an enterprise?

"Where are the boundaries?" we asked Abelino Aramayo, son of the owner.

"From the main road to the top of the mountain," he replied while pointing with his chin. "And from the river on Lacoyo side to Sullcata, the neighboring communities." With pride he showed titles dating back to Queen Isabella of Spain.

We nodded. It belonged to royalty at one time, but now boundaries could be tricky since they included mountain tops reaching 14,000 feet altitude, a river, a pile of rocks, a knobby knoll, and tufts of stiff wiry grass.

"Thirty *peons* are included in the price," he pressed his sale. "Good workers. You can't run a farm without them."

As we sat at a grimy table sipping strong black coffee from questionable demitasse cups, we learned that 30 *peons* meant 30 families, which translated into 146 persons. Our heads spun! Did we want a farm with 30 semi-slaves? Would we enjoy enforcing serf system rules? Frankly, we didn't know anything about serfdom.

As we walked around the compound, however, we became impressed. The one-hundred-year-old thatched farmhouse, with *tapial* walls, two-foot-thick pressed dirt, forming rooms around an open patio, could be used for a Bible School dorm, dining room, kitchen, and classrooms. Rooms left over would make a nice apartment for missionaries. A small, tile swimming pool almost filled the patio but certainly wasn't a selling point on the cold 12,500 foot *altiplano*.

An ancient Catholic church stood at the corner of the patio house, as we called this old hacienda house. This could be made into a nice chapel for the school and a Friends church for the community.

The red tile farmhouse, with a questionable bathroom and no septic tank, would also need a kitchen, something besides the windowless, smoky corner inhabited by guinea pigs where *peons* prepared the owners' meals.

Beautiful *huallata*, Andean snow geese, swam on the lake in the compound. In the evening fish jumped from its murky waters to catch insects.

A duck house, the gate house, and several sheds completed the buildings in the compound. Various trees—eucalyptus, scrawny stunted evergreens, seedling cherries, Russian olives, and willows—lined terraces, marked the driveway, and guarded houses and compound gates.

A high *tapial* wall marching around the compound to keep out animals and intruders did not bar the view. As we would learn later, nearby Mt. Ch'illa, slicing into the deep blue sky, provided the backdrop for colorful and thundering orchestrations of nature. It was also the scene of boundary disputes and a safe haven for thieves.

Down below and across the river a red sandstone cliff rose to provide not only a landmark but temptation for aspiring young cliff climbers. On across the pampa, about five miles, one could see famous Lake Titicaca. The hills of Peru lay beyond.

As we drove back to town we agreed that Copajira had possibilities for the location of a Bible School. Praying for God's direction, we advised the Mission Board in the States of its virtues as well as its drawbacks, then waited. What a happy day when we received the "go" sign, cashed a $23,740 check and paid for the farm, Copajira, with a suitcase of Bolivian money!

With exchange at 59 bolivianos to the dollar, Howard, Ralph, and Roscoe waited and watched for more than two hours while the teller counted 1,400,000 bolivianos—bundle after bundle of tattered money.

On February 7, 1947, we Knights loaded personal things into the new International pickup for the trip to the farm. The record-breaking rains that year had turned the roads to mud and water. We jolted from one mudhole to another, then sat beside the Colorado River for two hours until water subsided enough for us to ford. Five hours farther down the road we arrived at Rio Ch'illa where we waited again for the river to recede so we could ford.

Arriving at the farm, we found the former owner had not moved out as he promised. We also discovered he had not told the *peons* he had sold the farm and that we were the new owners. So Roscoe began his first day at Copajira dealing with some sticky issues. First, he insisted that Aramayo introduce us to the *peons* as the new owners. Next, he went to Guaqui, contracted a truck, helped Aramayo load his things (including a hand-grenade which we found in a drawer, and a sub-machine gun), and bid him good-bye as he departed for La Paz, leaving the place in a mess.

That night we spread our sleeping bags on the wood floor, and while the mice danced circles around and over us, we slept fitfully, wondering about the custom of Aymara *peons* bowing and addressing us as "*Mi Patrón.*"

Before leaving La Paz the missionary men had loaded furniture for both Pearsons and us into a boxcar, which the railroad company left on the siding on the northern boundary of the farm. From there we would bring everything two miles to the compound. We worked frantically to clean out all the debris before the furniture arrived.

"What do I do with this?" I held up a tattered old doll from a shelf in the living room.

"Throw it into the fireplace. We'll burn all that junk, if the fireplace works."

It did. Later we cleaned out the ashes and threw them over the compound wall. We didn't realize that we had thrown those ashes in the main path people used when going to their fields or to town.

Early next morning a group arrived at our kitchen door to ask for the key so they could enter the church "to confess." The mission council had decided we would not open the church for Catholic services but we would help them build another building outside the compound up near their homes, so we denied their request.

Soon they came back. "Please, Patrón, we'd like to take the saints out of the church." We gladly gave them the huge eight-inch iron key to the heavy colonial door of the church.

As we watched, they filed out the back gate, carrying images, candles, pictures, and other items used in worship. We felt the Lord had solved the problem of our having to clean out the church. But we didn't know the whole story.

"Why did they take the saints out of the church?" Roscoe asked José, our 13 year old Aymara helper.

"They think you will burn them," José explained.

Later we learned one of the women had found the ashes we'd thrown over the wall, and in it she spied a piece of metallic lace that hadn't burned. She spread the word that we were burning the saints.

"Uh-huh, now we know. That shelf in the living room wall is an altar, a place for images and candles," Roscoe explained as we examined the shelf.

"And the doll we burned was not a doll at all," I added. "It was an image minus a leg, with metallic lace on the dress." We had much to learn about the customs of these Aymara people and the methods of handling touchy situations. Looking back we can see the Lord's protection as we blundered through many dangerous situations. We're sure He protected us, for we made many mistakes while learning the rules of serfdom and the customs of the Aymara people.

In the 1500's when Pizarro rode in to conquer Peru and Bolivia, he also brought with him from Spain the Roman Catholic religion and serfdom, a system of slavery. Spanish nobles divided Bolivia into large acreages, which they called *haciendas*. Aymaras, even though they had lived on the land for centuries, were considered *peons*, property of the *hacienda*. Being virtually slaves of the landowner, they were forced to work several days a week for the privilege of living on and farming a small plot. The owner usually gave them the rocky ground while keeping the best land for himself. He also felt it beneath his dignity to do any work so forced the *peons* to be shepherds, cheese makers, farmers, bakers, cooks, or do whatever needed to be done. When the mission bought Copajira, they bought this kind of a situation, acquiring 30 families of *peons*.

In days ahead the *peons* found it difficult to adjust to their new owner. The first week we began making changes. When we found that two *peons* had to milk over 100 sheep twice a day for enough milk to make only one cheese every night, which sold for only 15 cents, we canceled cheese-making. Common sense told us that healthy lambs would be worth more than 15 cents a day. The time spent milking sheep and weaving *jichu*, a wiry grass, into cheese molds could be spent in more worthwhile projects.

We also changed the custom of giving alcohol and *coca* leaves to the *peons* after work each day. This age-old custom undoubtedly began because *coca* is a narcotic that deadens the pangs of hunger. Since both *coca* and alcohol are sacred to the Aymara and used in their animistic rituals, they thought it a necessity. They weren't happy when we gave them bread and sugar instead of alcohol and *coca*, but they learned to accept it.

We made another change that could have caused serious consequences. We changed a boundary in order to settle a dispute. Boundary disputes, common between farms, happened because people living on the farms had such small plots they took land from their neighbors if they could get away with it. They used a grassy knoll or large clump of wiry grass for boundary markers. Over the years or sometimes overnight, these changed slightly, causing feuds between farms. This situation occurred between us and Lacoyo, our neighboring farm to the east, so we tried to settle the dispute.

For years the men from both Copajira and Lacoyo fought over boundaries, resulting in the death of one

Lacoyo man. We didn't like all the fighting so consulted the ancient map included with the titles, which showed that Copajira *peons* were farming on Lacoyo land. Roscoe signed a peace agreement with the administrator of Lacoyo, putting the boundary back where it should be according to the map. This made Copajira *peons* furious.

Roscoe outlined the work for the *peons* one morning. "Today you will build a *tapial* wall to mark the boundary here along this disputed area between Lacoyo and Copajira." They refused. He insisted, literally pushing some to work. Several grumbled and all looked sullen. After a tense time they built the wall. Here again God protected, for the *peons* could have easily stoned Roscoe. Today, much wiser, he would be afraid to do such a thing, but it paid rich dividends.

"*Hermano* Raúl (Roscoe), I came to know the Lord Jesus because you provided a just and honest settlement of that boundary dispute," Esteban Roque of Lacoyo said years later.

The *peons* didn't like change. Neither did they like us because we were Protestants. Our honesty made them angry. Since the land had been theirs for centuries they thought they could do as they pleased. This caused problems.

Roscoe had problems adjusting to being go-between, peacemaker, doctor, and tough guy. I wrote to our family in the States:

Tuesday one of our *peons* came to report that our neighbors on the farm to the west were farming across the boundary on our land. Wednesday another man came saying a neighbor had stolen land up in the hills. Also, that day two husbands brought their wives to settle a quarrel. Thursday a *peón* came saying another man was living with his wife—could we please do something about it? And today a fellow came saying one of our *peons* was in jail in Guaqui because he got in a fight when he was drunk. What a life! The Aymaras have little clout with public officials so they consider Roscoe their "go-between" and peacemaker.

The following week we had to deal with Crisóstomo who lived with another man's wife. Crisóstomo was *jilacata* of Copajira. Every farm had a *jilacata*, a head man responsible for tending to the *peons'* official business. When government officials in Guaqui, the county seat, heard about Crisóstomo's problem they said he should be punished because of his bad example in the community.

How do you punish such a crime? We called all the *peons* together to explain the situation. "We must appoint another *jilacata*. Which one of you would like to be the official representative for Copajira?"

No one wanted the position and everyone wanted Crisóstomo to continue in office. Roscoe felt that he should be punished in some way for his actions, so he asked for Crisóstomo's *jilacata's* stick and black poncho. The stick, a symbol of authority, was of highly polished black wood with decorated bands of silver around it and a short leather whip attached.

Crisóstomo fell on his knees at Roscoe's feet. "Please, *Patrón*, don't take them. Don't take them," he begged through sobs.

Many farm owners and administrators used a *chicote*, a blacksnake whip, to force *peons* to obey. Aymara men carried a *chicote* over the shoulder and used them for controlling their animals, wives, and children. Roscoe didn't think it right to use such methods so took the *jilacata's* stick and poncho from Crisóstomo. A humiliated Crisóstomo walked out the back gate, up the hill to his house.

That evening Máximo, one of our workers from La Paz, explained the importance of the *jilacata's* stick and poncho.

"Pastor, the *jilacata's* stick and black poncho are sacred. The *jilacata* is never without them. He sleeps in the poncho and always carries the stick. The Aymara believes that if he takes them off, the gods will destroy the crops or bring some destruction to the land."

Roscoe didn't sleep well that night. He'd made another "boo-boo" but hoped that Crisóstomo had learned his lesson. Next morning he returned those sacred objects to a happy *peón* who again fell at Roscoe's feet and grabbed him around the knees, but this time he shed tears of joy.

Along with being an arbitrator, Roscoe also doctored the sick. During a fiesta two *peons* got into a fight, resulting in a deep gash in one man's head. Angry, and spitting words, they both came to the house for medicine.

"Here," Roscoe said, handing each a swab saturated with Mercurochrome. "Take these and each of you can doctor the other fellow." Astonished, they obeyed and left smiling when they finished.

Some illnesses involved witchcraft, of which we knew almost nothing. "*Buenos días, mi patrón,*" a *peón* bowed to greet Roscoe one morning. "My daughter is dying. Do you have some medicine?"

"Let's go see what's the matter, Lorenzo."

With Lorenzo leading the way, Roscoe and José climbed the hill to their straw-thatched adobe house above our compound. As they entered a patio surrounded by a low rock wall, a mangy black dog greeted them with a growl then slunk away when Lorenzo picked up a rock. "She's in there," Lorenzo tilted his chin to indicate a hut on one side of the patio.

Roscoe bent low to enter a dark musty room. After a few seconds, his eyes adjusting to the darkness, on a mud platform covered with sheep hides under heavy coarse homespun wool blankets, he saw the form of a young girl about 16 years old curled in a fetal position with her face to the wall.

"Where do you hurt?" Roscoe asked when he knew she had no fever, no cough or cold, didn't spit blood and had no outward signs of any disease such as chicken pox, smallpox, scarlet fever, or measles. She shook her head. She didn't hurt. Obviously she was wasting away.

"Pastor," José whispered to Roscoe when he went out into the patio. "Lorenzo just told me that she has been cursed by the witch doctor from Lacoyo. A fellow from Lacoyo wanted to marry her but she refused so he hired the witch doctor to put a curse on her. That's the reason she's sick."

Apparently the girl wanted to starve herself to death. With the authority of the farm owner Roscoe tackled the situation.

"I demand that you get out of that bed and eat some food. I have more power than the witch doctor and expect you to be back at work soon."

"Fix some chicken soup for her," he instructed the mother, "and put her out in the sunshine."

Without Roscoe's intervention undoubtedly she would have died from fear and lack of food. Within a few weeks, however, she came back to work.

Witch doctors often practiced their incantations on people near us. One day a young girl came into the patio of the old farmhouse. Julia Pearson listened to her story.

"My brother got drunk at a fiesta and bit me on my temple," she explained. "It didn't get well so I went to the witch doctor. After he charged me a chicken and put some medicine on the sore it became worse. Now I have come to you."

An angry red indicated a definite infection. Julia cleaned away the dried *coca* leaves that stuck to the sore. "What's that?" Roscoe asked as he stood by to take a lesson on mopping up a botched witch doctor job. "It looks like there's something black in it."

Sure enough, Julia used her tweezers and pulled out a piece of meat about an inch long. "It's a guinea pig tendon," she exclaimed. Then she promptly filled the wound with sulfa powder and a happy girl left the compound.

One evening a leathery looking *peón* came with a unique problem. "*Señor*, I have something wrong with my ear. I have a train in here." Luís explained, as he shook his head and turned his ear up. "Hear it? Hear it?"

"You have a what? A train?" Of course Roscoe couldn't hear anything but went for his otoscope. Upon examination, he saw a tick attached to the eardrum. With extreme care he extracted the offender and the train didn't bother Luís anymore.

Some problems were more difficult to solve. Thievery at harvest time was a way of life, as we learned our first year on Copajira. To harvest potatoes Aymara men drove a yoke of oxen pulling a wooden plow down the potato rows, while women sifted through the dirt, lifted the potatoes to fill their baskets, then dumped them in piles. They sometimes hid the bigger potatoes in their private packs, which they carried on their backs, or buried them and came back at night to dig them again. Our larger potatoes found their way to 30 homes each night, leaving us with marble-sized ones. One of the more honest *peons* advised us of this, so one evening when the workers came to the house for bread Roscoe asked to see in each person's pack. There he found the largest of our potatoes, only about golf ball size that first year.

To teach the *peons* the consequences of thievery Roscoe required that two from each family come to work the next day. They refused. So he demanded they all work four days instead of the usual three. It seemed they could never learn that this new *patrón* was a hard taskmaster if they didn't play fair.

When they let their animals feed on our barley we caught one of their sheep, took it to Guaqui, and left it with the *corregidor* (local policeman). They had to pay a fine to get their sheep back. But even though it cost them they continued to pasture our fields.

"Why are you taking the fertilizer from our sheep corral?" our farm administrator asked a peón woman. "That's stealing and that's wrong."

"No," she defended her actions, "it's daytime so it isn't stealing."

Lying and stealing, their way of life, was as natural for the *peons* as breathing. They cut our barley before it ripened; dug our potatoes and picked our *habas* at night or when we weren't watching. They dug a hole through the wall to steal our pigs, and traded their sickly sheep for our large healthy merinos. The shepherd absconded with forty large merino sheep but the law was on his side since we could prove nothing. They also stole our llamas before we ever knew we had any.

One week when co-worker Jack Willcuts needed the pickup to make a trip to Amacari, he and Gerry rode the train to Guaqui. We were just going to bed when someone tapped on the bedroom window.

"Anyone home?" Jack called.

They had walked seven miles from Guaqui to spend the night with us and take the pickup back to La Paz the next day.

The day Jack brought the vehicle back we encouraged them to stay a day or two, to rest up a bit.

"I'd like to hike to the back of the farm," Roscoe said. "Come go with me."

A steady climb took them up, up, up the mountain to an altitude of over 14,000 feet, around boulders where the wild *viscachas* hid, over rock terraces built in pre-Inca times. Sometimes the men followed a rocky trail and other times they struck out across the mountain, past clumps of emerald green lichen, blue lupine, or tiny daisies hugging the ground but always being careful to avoid the sticky *jichu* grass used to thatch roofs. Roscoe hoped the exhilarating climb would help minimize farm problems.

"What did you find?" I asked when the men arrived home about suppertime.

"It was a profitable trip," Roscoe answered. "We found about a thousand sheep from Jesús de Machaca grazing on our land. We also found several families from across the mountain moving in on our property, and our own *peons* are farming up there."

"We found llamas, too," Jack added.

"What's this about llamas?" I asked at the supper table.

"Do you remember when the peons asked for a sheep for a barbecue after they finished building our school building?"

I nodded.

"Well, when I didn't give them one, they had their barbecue anyway," Roscoe explained. "I didn't pay any attention but they barbecued a llama instead of a lamb. And what's more, it was our llama. Evidently Rufino has had our llamas hidden up on the mountain ever since we bought the farm. We brought down five big ones and two babies."

"What did you do with them?"

"We put them in the chicken pen. Tomorrow I'll let the shepherd run them with the sheep."

"I do declare," I slowly shook my head, "we have to tie down everything on this farm to keep it from walking off!"

After supper Knights and Willcutses played Rook, the boys entertained us with jokes from <u>Reader's Digest</u> and we all tried to forget our problems.

"I'll sure be glad when Cammacks get here," Roscoe said as we trailed off to bed. "It will be good when Paul takes over the farm. I don't like confrontation. I sure hope he does. I'll help him if he wants it but I'd rather work in the Bible School." "I hope the work isn't as demanding when they arrive," I continued the conversation as we snuggled into a cold bed in July. "I'm afraid you won't be able to take time off for the arrival of our new baby." We had one more new experience to face that year. "I'm scared, but I'll be more scared if you're not with me when the baby is born."

"Don't worry. I'll be there." And he was.

Gary Dean arrived on November 8, 1947, but he didn't come into this world screaming, or even breathing. The doctor quickly gave him to Elvira Firestone, a missionary nurse who was with me.

"I took him into the next room," Elvira told us later. "I did everything I knew to get him to breathe, but he would not respond. I was frantic. I prayed as I worked and finally he caught a breath. I didn't leave him until late that evening. I know that boy is alive today because of the Lord's touch," she concluded with a husky voice and tears in her eyes.

After I spent ten days in a hospital bed, as was Latin custom, we braved muddy roads and swollen rivers to get back to our home on Copajira.

Copajira—Mission Farm

Suitcase of money for the farm purchase.

Copajira Jilacata

4

POSSESSION BUT
NO PEACE

Tradition dictated that we "take possession" of the land when we first moved to Copajira. We postponed this ceremony until the arrival of Paul and Phyllis Cammack and their three children, David, Daniel, and MaryBel. We wanted the *peons* and surrounding communities to recognize *don* Pablo (Paul) as the *patrón*, owner of the farm. In later years Leland Hibbs became *patrón*, but Aymaras are steeped in tradition, making it difficult for them to change. To the end they considered *don* Raúl (Roscoe) the *patrón* since we were the ones who bought the farm and lived there first. No legal ceremony could change their minds.

"Where did you get that scruffy burro?" I asked as I glanced out the kitchen window one morning to see the animal tied to the wind generator in our yard.

"That's a mule," Roscoe corrected me, "Victoriano brought him this morning. I'm going to Guaqui after

34

breakfast to bring out the Judge and his secretary. They'll need something to ride. They say they can't walk to the top of the mountain."

"Jack and you climbed to the top not long ago," I half argued. Somehow I always felt the officials were trying to take advantage of us.

"I know, but these fellows who work in offices aren't used to such strenuous exercise. In fact, they said they wouldn't help us `take possession' of the farm unless we provided transportation."

"Do you mean that both men will ride on that one poor little donkey?" Now I defended the donkey.

Later that morning I watched as the Judge, mounted on the farm pony, and the secretary, riding on the mule, rode out the back gate then started their ascent to mark Copajira's boundaries. Paul, Howard, Roscoe, and about 40 *peons* climbed with them.

The procession wound its way along the boundaries marked by piles of rocks, mounds of earth, tufts of *jichu*, mountain peaks, river, and cliffs. The Judge and his secretary dismounted at important boundary markers to deliver speeches and read the proper documents. The missionaries performed the traditional ritual of rolling over on the ground at the corners of the property while the *peons* showered them with confetti and orange peelings. The pageantry of the occasion duly impressed the Bolivians.

The grapevine carried news of the "*gringos*" of Copajira "taking possession," so neighboring communities were alert to any encroachment on their property. Since Roscoe had already settled the dispute with Lacoyo, everything went smoothly along the border to the east. A large community beyond the mountain, Jesús de Machaca, however, disputed the line hotly, for they saw their grazing area disappearing. Then Sullcata on our west proved to be the biggest challenge. Here the pageantry of the occasion evaporated into the rare air.

High on the mountain, some 14,000 feet high, where Sullcata, Jesús de Machaca, and Copajira met, a large group of Sullcata drunks stood their ground when the Copajira delegation approached the peak marking the boundary.

"Stop! Don't come any closer," they yelled. "This is our land."

"No, the hill behind you is the boundary," Juan, a Copajira *peón*, yelled.

"They're drunk," someone muttered. "We can't reason with a bunch of drunks."

But still some insisted they were on our land. Copajira *peons* didn't want to give up one inch of land.

As the argument got louder, some *peons* shoved the intruders, and rocks began to fly. The Judge and his secretary spurred their animals off down the mountain, with the missionaries in hot pursuit.

Roscoe looked back to see Juan had advanced closer, insisting on his rights to the land, but soon he too came flying down the mountain in a shower of rocks.

A few days later, with soldiers for protection, the Judge came back to finish the ceremony. All went smoothly and the three missionary men rolled over on the grass in our yard while the *peons* showered them with flower petals.

"Taking possession" of a farm is definitely a part of the Aymara culture but this bit of ceremony proved dangerous and did not solve all our problems. In fact, it reinforced the resistance of the *peons* to these Protestant missionaries.

The government encouraged every farm to maintain a primary school. Since the school was held inside the farm compound we built a new school building up toward the hills near the *peons'* homes and hired a new teacher. We refused to pay for a government teacher who would teach religion. If the *peons* wanted a government teacher, they would have to pay him.

Peons brought the *Intendente* (sheriff) from Guaqui thinking he would force us to pay for whomever they chose as teacher but Roscoe stood firm. "We will provide a school building. We will provide a teacher. But we reserve the right to choose the teacher." With all their arguing, the *Intendente* and *peons* could not change the situation so went away with plans to take the matter to higher authorities.

"We'll fight for a school of our own religion," they threatened.

Four fellows kept much of the trouble bubbling. One had killed a *peón* on a neighboring farm. Another, a squatter, tried to take a widow's property. A third, the secretary of education, was supposed to settle school problems, not cause them. All joined the fourth, determined to remove Protestants from their farm.

The four troublemakers, angry when they heard of the possibility of their being forced to leave the farm, stirred an already tense situation one evening at the end of a working day when we passed out bread.

"Now that we're all here," one suggested, "let's fight 'em."

Students at the Bible School, in session at that time, became frightened when they heard the comment. That night they either heard or imagined men walking outside their window but were too scared to come tell us.

A few days later we made the trip to La Paz to talk to our lawyer, that indispensable authority in Bolivia.

"I told the *Intendente* what we would do to cooperate with the *peons*, but he did not want to listen," Roscoe concluded his explanation of the situation.

"Don't worry about it," Miranda shrugged his shoulders while turning his palms up. "It's no big deal. There's no law in the land that can force you to provide a school to their specifications."

Back at the farm, Roscoe, wanting to be fair with the *peons*, offered them their choice of two pieces of land upon which they could build a school building, but they refused the offer.

"Pastor," student Casimero called as he hobbled up to Roscoe, "from out behind the compound I notice someone has raised a flag on the school building." Casimero knew we had been having trouble with the *peons* over the school situation.

Saturday morning with no classes in session, we hiked up to the school. *Peons* scattered when they saw us coming. On the ridge of the roof someone had planted a cross made of straw as their sign of ownership.

"It looks like they are taking over the building," someone commented. "Let's see if we can knock that cross off." After several misses, a rock made a direct hit, knocking it flat. Later that afternoon we hung a padlock on the door.

The following Saturday night *peons* broke the glassless window frames. They also knocked a hole in the door, large enough for a man to crawl through, and ruined the padlock.

We feared this defiance. *Peons* near Sucre, a city south of La Paz, stoned the owner of their farm to death about that time. Such news sweeping across the altiplano didn't make us feel comfortable.

"We're having trouble sleeping since the *peons* have become so defiant," I wrote home to our folks in the States. "We're always hearing things outside our window, but maybe it is just our imagination. Anyway, we don't like the thought of a stick of dynamite being flung through our bedroom window some night."

A short time later public schools opened, so we removed the new padlock, hired a teacher, and prayed for peace and quiet. But all too soon the teacher knocked at our door.

"*Don* Raúl, some fellow came to the school and claimed to be the teacher. He just took over. I had to leave."

"Come with me," Roscoe said. They jumped into the truck, picking up Paul as they drove out the back gate. "Evidently Saturnino Choque is back insisting he is the teacher. What shall we do with him?"

With only a short ride to the school they didn't have time to discuss the situation but promptly went into action.

"What's going on here?" Roscoe asked.

"I'm the teacher here," Saturnino retorted. "The fathers on this farm are satisfied with my teaching and I'm here to stay."

"You were fired, so go," Roscoe ordered.

When he showed no inclination to leave, Paul forcefully helped him into the pickup, and they drove back down to the compound.

"Sign here," Roscoe said as he handed him a pen.

Reluctantly, Saturnino signed a statement saying he would not be back to molest the school nor the *peons* again. Then they took him two miles to the main road, let him off and told him never to come back.

Getting rid of that teacher, however, did not solve all our problems. In fact, it may have caused a few.

When we bought the farm, one member of each family worked three days a week for the farm for the privilege of farming a plot of land for themselves. The day they plowed land for the farm they marked the acreage into 30 sections with a *peón* being responsible for plowing each section.

Plowing was a memorable sight. Aymaras in ponchos followed teams of oxen pulling wooden plows to scratch the rocky soil of the *altiplano*. Some oxen wore mirrors on their foreheads to frighten away evil spirits while others had colorful Bolivian flags waving from their yokes behind the horns.

Oxen and the wooden plow are indispensable tools for Aymara farmers. With them they plow the land, they make rows for planting, and they dig the potatoes at harvest time. The *chunta*, however, a short-handled hoe, is also necessary for cultivating and finishing the potato harvest. Farmers use a sickle or the sharpened edge of a tin can to cut barley, then pile it into golden shocks and cover them with freshly pulled *quinoa* stalks so the birds can't eat the grain. Finally, they pull and stack *haba* stalks, the English broad bean.

Threshing time follows harvest. Men flay the grain and beans with long sticks, then throw it into the air where the wind carries away the chaff. After pouring the grain into homespun gunnysacks, they load the sacks on a burro to carry them home for storage in the corner of the kitchen or bedroom.

We watched the *peons* plow, plant, and harvest, then realized we'd have to mechanize if we hoped to make Copajira profitable. We bought a small Farmall A tractor, the largest one available in Bolivia at that time. For generations those living on the farm had plowed, planted, and harvested, but now machinery did the job. No one knows how the *peons* felt about this impersonal piece of iron but evidently they didn't entirely trust it for they still performed some of their rituals for better crops. When potatoes began to bloom, *peons* gathered in the fields to pay *Pachamama*, the goddess of the earth. Though animists they relied on a Christian symbol and planted a small wooden cross in each field. After the ritual of killing a rooster, they sprinkled the blood around the field, showered each other with confetti, then sprinkled alcohol throughout the field and drank what was left. Thus, the goddess of the earth would, supposedly, give them a good crop that year.

After Cammacks arrived Paul was named the official farmer and added other implements: plow, drill, combine, and the larger Farmall M tractor. With every purchase we lessened the burden of work for the *peons*, and also improved living conditions in the compound.

Primitive living conditions on Copajira forced us to seek solutions. Water arrived at the compound by an open ditch from the hills above but we were skeptical of its purity so dug a well, thinking we could have clean water. Even though we dug fifty yards from the lake we soon discovered lake water in our "oaken bucket." Eventually Paul and his brother, Forrest, solved the problem by piping water from the hills above. Nationals marvelled at being able to turn on a faucet for a drink of water or to wash their dusty feet and legs after working in the fields. With no electricity we used candles, kerosene lanterns, or an Aladdin lamp for a more elegant look. Eventually a five- kilowatt diesel generator made life easier for everyone living in the compound.

To provide a better diet we planted a vegetable garden. Frost, hail, and thieves proved to be enemies of the garden. Frost attacked by night, hail by day, and thieves when missionaries weren't there to guard it.

Julia, Phyllis, and I loved flowers, but again we fought the elements. After the *peons* filled the swimming pool in the patio with dirt, we had a protected place for a garden: snapdragons, pinks, poppies, iris, delphinium, stocks, pansies, and many others. I even planted sweet peas in wooden nail kegs along the warmer south wall. But with all our care, sometimes the weather won the battle.

"I feel like Job," Julia moaned after a severe hailstorm swept across the compound. "I'm going back to La Paz." At the moment she had forgotten that hail also falls in La Paz. Fortunately our crops weren't touched that year, even though we had hail five days in one week.

Problems of water, electricity, and gardens were simple in comparison to those of the farm. One day when Paul went down to grease the combine and finish threshing barley, he discovered two peon women taking bundles of barley.

"Hey, get out of the barley," he yelled across the field.

They immediately started throwing rocks at him. Two rocks hit him, and since he didn't know much Spanish, he went back to the house seeking Roscoe's help.

As Roscoe strode across the barley field he hollered, "Scram! Get out of here." A rock flew his way but he marched up to the woman, daring her to throw more.

Scared and angry, she dropped to the ground and started hitting herself on the head with a rock.

"Get into the pickup," Roscoe ordered. "We're going to the police." They wouldn't budge.

Other farm owners enforced the law with the *chicote*, a long whip, but he couldn't do that. So he and Paul lifted the women's hats from their heads and taking the bundles of barley they had in their *ahuayos*, packs on their backs, they drove off to Guaqui to leave the evidence with the police.

"I know they will go for their hats," Roscoe said, "and I also know they will have to pay a fine to get their hats and for stealing the barley. We just hope they learn a lesson."

Tradition dictated that with every piece of land the *peons* plowed and planted for the farm, they got a piece of similar size to plant for themselves. When we plowed with the tractor the *peons* felt cheated so we offered to give them their own land with titles. They refused. They kept asking for more land to plant, even stole land, but they didn't want to own it.

"*Señor*," the *Jilacata* spoke for the *peons*, "we'd like to plant that piece of land across the river."

"No," Paul answered, "you can't have that land. I'll plow that with the tractor and we'll plant it to potatoes. You can't plant there. If you do, I'll disk it under."

They understood but went away disgruntled.

Later on Saturday night 30 *peons* with 30 teams of oxen and plows silently gathered on our best land down on the pampa. They plowed and sowed 20 acres with *quinoa*.

On October 22, 1948, La Paz celebrated the 400th anniversary of its founding. Officials planned a big celebration. Sensing tension, they called in all the soldiers from surroundering towns to help keep the peace.

"Do all you can to keep your *peons* happy these days," the Sheriff cautioned Roscoe when he reported the illegal planting of *quinoa*. "We won't have any police protection here in Guaqui now. There could be an uprising."

The national celebration came and went with no revolution in the city and towns but rumors and private uprisings sprung up in country areas.

"Kill all the *patróns* and change all the *haciendas* into communities," ordered communist agitators.

"We'll kill the missionaries and hang them on their own trees," one of our *peons* bragged.

The missionaries felt insecure. All three fellows, Paul, Howard, and Roscoe, had shotguns or .22 and .30-.30 rifles, and Roscoe had a .22 caliber revolver, which he occasionally wore on his hip under his coat. He had never used the revolver for anything except target practice and shooting birds on Lake Titicaca.

"I couldn't shoot anyone," he commented, "but I could scare him away."

Before the celebration and upon hearing of suspected trouble, the menfolk decided to bring out more weapons from La Paz.

"Perhaps the size of our arsenal might deter any problems," they reasoned.

On Sunday night as we prepared for bed, we heard a light tap on our window.

"Pastor Raúl," Máximo called. "Come quick."

"*Qué pasa*, what's the matter?"

"Look, the *peons* are signaling with fires on the mountain," Máximo pointed up behind the compound and talked faster than his usual slow drawl. "They're sending a message to Lacoyo. They're going to attack."

Frightened believers soon surrounded us, all talked at once and everyone gave different advice. We didn't know it at the time but heard later that the people had used fires to signal for an attack during a revolution several years earlier.

"Let's all go to the chapel." There we read Psalm 91, sang, prayed, and sang again until all felt calm.

"Let's divide into three groups," someone suggested. "We'll take turns walking around the compound all night."

We had a peaceful sleep that night but read Psalm 91 for three more nights. Not knowing whether to expect dynamite to come flying through our bedroom window or that we might be hung on our own trees, we prayed that God would take away the fear and give us peace. He did.

A week later with things back to normal in the government, peace prevailed on the farm. Or so we thought, until we discovered the *quinoa* the *peons* had planted on our land had sprouted—just when we wanted to plant potatoes.

A young Bible School boy had learned to drive the tractor so offered to disk under the *quinoa*. Roscoe and Paul stood guard, not knowing what to expect.

They hadn't been in the field long when *peons* started gathering. Seeing the situation, the men knew they would need help so Roscoe jumped into the Jeep, sped off to Guaqui and came back with two soldiers.

"I don't want to disk anymore." Filemón, face a pasty white, jumped down from the tractor, refusing to face the crowd.

"I'll do it," Paul offered and started around the field. All was calm. *Peons* feared to attack.

At just that moment a carload of Americans stopped along the main road. "We're lost. Can you tell us how to get to Sorata?"

"You <u>are</u> lost," Roscoe said. "This is a long way out of your way. You have to go back to...," and he explained in detail.

"We're also thirsty," one mentioned. "Would you happen to have any boiled water."

Roscoe took note and saw everything under control—Paul disking, the soldiers standing nearby, and the *peons* calmly watching.

"Sure, follow me to the house. We've got plenty of water."

As soon as he left, the women picked up rocks. They waited until Paul went over a rise and down into a hollow where he couldn't be seen by the soldiers, then attacked.

Soldiers ran to the rescue but refused to use force so the women continued stoning Paul. Before the soldiers quieted things several rocks hit and Paul's hand had swollen from severe bruises.

When Roscoe arrived, he found the soldiers too scared to enforce order, so again he went to Guaqui to obtain an order for all the *peons* to appear before the police. The Sheriff put eight *peons* in jail and sent four soldiers out to keep order until we finished disking. It was a tense time, both for frightened believers living in the compound and for the missionaries.

The following month we invited the Lieutenant-Governor, head of the police in our state, to talk to the peons. They turned down everything we offered until the authorities insisted they should accept our Freedom Plan. Nineteen finally accepted freedom, their own land with titles, but the older *peons* refused to change.

We also gave them land on the west side for their own school and church. The Lieutenant-Governor forced them to sign papers saying they would no longer press for our school and church buildings inside our compound. A defeat for the *peons* signaled the end of a long tedious battle. At last we had hopes there would be peace on Copajira. Now we trusted the Bible School program could advance without interruption, since that was the reason we had purchased Copajira in the first place.

Plowing with a yoke of oxen.

A Peon home on Copajira

5

BIBLE SCHOOL

In 1932, Helen Cammack, a newly appointed Friends missionary, arrived in Bolivia. She fell in love with the Aymara people and became their beloved teacher as she directed and taught in schools. Countless times she rode her faithful mule, Yanapiri (Helper), across Puerto Perez/Pucarani/Batallas pampa distributing tracts and teaching the Scriptures in humble thatched adobe homes. She became one with the Aymaras. When typhoid fever took her after only two terms on the field the Aymara brethren asked for a Bible School. Señorita Elena had whetted their appetites for studying the Scriptures.

One month after we moved to Copajira—March 1947—the Helen Cammack Memorial Bible Training School opened for classes.

Howard and Julia Pearson had also returned from furlough to teach in the school. With small faith, we made limited preparations that year. However, four girls and nine fellows arrived for the first week and four more came later—seventeen students, eager to learn. But some were not capable.

The first year studies were simple. A few students could barely read and write so had to have special help, while four or five had finished the third grade and spoke Spanish well. The following years we added more courses: Doctrine, Child Evangelism, Bible Geography, and Homiletics. Some students also became involved in drama, chorus, and private organ lessons.

Since Aymaras only sang the melody, a year or two later Roscoe and Phyllis struggled to teach 27 students to sing in harmony. They divided the group and each group learned its part. Repetition, the key to learning in Bolivia, proved a success when they sang parts together. Presto, it sounded beautiful!

Others, wanting to learn a trade, took advantage of studying carpentry, tailoring, or hat making. Since most students came from country areas they had a hands-on education in farming and animal husbandry. They learned how to fertilize their fields and plant larger seed potatoes to produce larger potatoes. They watched as better breeding stock produced healthier lambs.

The students also learned much about their own animistic culture. Many afternoons a dark cloud appeared from behind Mt. Ch'illa. All across the pampa smoke from little grass fires ascended in the still air. Soon we heard the high shrill calls to the hail god, "*Achachila, pasanimaya*" (grandfather god, pass over our crops). Sometimes they called, "*Lunthat achachila, pasanimaya"* (old robber grandfather god, pass over our crops).

"*Señor*," Hilarión panted, having run from a field below the house, "the witch doctor from Lacoyo is down in our barley field. He's putting a curse on it so the hail will destroy our barley."

"Don't worry, Hilarión," Roscoe tried to calm him, "he can't destroy our crop. We'll trust in God to take care of it."

Sometimes the *peons* went to Guaqui to hire a witch doctor to protect their own crops, but evidently this time they had hired a witch doctor from our neighboring farm to destroy ours.

Sure enough, that afternoon an angry cloud arose over Ch'illa. Aymaras started their grass fires, called to their hail god. It hailed. It left a white strip across the *peons'* fields, jumped our field of barley, and hailed on across the witchdoctor's fields in Lacoyo. The Bible School students learned a valuable lesson—a lesson in trusting in God's care.

While we taught Bible classes on Copajira, our neighboring farm, Lacoyo, trained witchdoctors. We suspected they often practiced their encantations on us.

"*Señor! Señor!* Come quickly!" Mama Luisa, the Bible School cook called at our bedroom window early one morning.

Roscoe dressed in a jiffy, sensing the urgency in her voice.

"Come see what I found when I came to put the water on for breakfast this morning." Luisa trotted ahead of him to the school kitchen. "There, don't touch it. Don't look in it," she warned, while pointing down at a clay basin in front of the kitchen door.

"Why?" Roscoe asked.

"It's been cursed," Luisa whispered with a frightened look. "If you see yourself in it you will die."

"I'm not afraid, Luisa. God will take care of us. We don't have to fear the witchdoctor." A student boldly picked up the basin, walked across the flower terrace to toss it over the wall.

The first hour class didn't spend time studying the life of Christ but discussed the practical issues of animism.

"Tell me about it," Roscoe encouraged the class.

"Evidently someone paid the *brujo*, witchdoctor, to put a curse on one of us in the patio," Máximo explained. "The belief is that if the *brujo* buys a new water basin, takes a bath and pours the water in the basin, then puts it in front of the door of the person he wants to destroy, and that person sees his reflection in the water, he will die."

They eagerly discussed witchcraft, fear, and how to trust the Lord, for all had grown up in an environment where witchcraft and fear were constant companions. Both students and missionaries learned new lessons every day.

Knights, Pearsons, and Cammacks taught in the school the first three years. Then as furloughs rotated missionary staff every year, others moved to the farm to teach in the school— Ralph and Marie Chapman, Leland and Iverna Hibbs, Marshal and Catherine Cavit, David and Florence Thomas, and Everett and Alda Clarkson.

After the first year the student body consisted of Aymara men between the ages of 15 and 40, mostly single, many with little or no formal education, some with little Spanish and all with no assets, thus the reason for working for their room and board.

The school grew every year. They came from La Paz, from the cordillera, from the peninsula beyond the Straits of Tiquina, from the area bordering Chile and Peru, and eventually they came from the Yungas, the lowlands on the eastern slopes of the Andes mountains.

The second year we saw the need for building small houses for the few married students. *Peons* and students made adobes and built small two-room houses outside the main compound.

Being low on funds, Roscoe wrote his father in the States. "Dad, you asked what you could do to help so we have a suggestion. We need doors and windows for the married student houses. It will cost about $50 a house—not much when we build of adobe and straw roofing."

Some married students with young children arrived in desperate straits financially. Babies, wrapped in rags, coughed and turned blue with the cold.

"Roscoe, would you please lift those sacks of rice and sugar off the clothes trunk in the storeroom?" I asked shortly after school started. "I have to find some clothes for those kids."

The Women's Missionary Union sent a supply of used clothing and baby layettes with every missionary coming to Bolivia. These items caused jealousy and sometimes serious problems but for the most part they met a real need, especially for Aymara children.

"A gown, a sweater, blanket and shirt," I counted. "That should do it for the baby. And these two sweaters for the two older kids."

I slammed the lid of the crate and went out behind the compound to the married students' houses to deliver the clothes. The dim dark room felt clammy and little tykes shivered in only tattered shirts. The little boy wore nothing below the waist for it was far easier not to have to wash diapers or pants.

The baby cried; the little ones coughed.

"Muchas gracias, hermana," Victoria said. I left, but I couldn't forget the scene.

The next day I heated water and invited Victoria in to my kitchen. I bathed the kids and they came out a few shades lighter. Then I rubbed Vaseline on their chapped cheeks, hands and feet, and Vicks Vaporub on all those who had coughs. Of course they all had coughs at the moment.

Sometimes we gave out more than Vicks Vaporub—worm capsules, *mejoral* (aspirin), and castor oil.

"Buenas noches, Señor," Eugenio greeted Roscoe as he answered a knock at the kitchen door. "We've come for medicine." He looked at his wife, Marcela, with a nod, as though to include her also.

"What kind of medicine? What do you need?"

"Marcela needs the same kind you gave Casimero's wife," Eugenio explained.

"Let's see..." Roscoe tried to remember, "Oh, you mean you need a purge," he finished, looking directly at Marcela.

"No, no, that's not it," Eugenio interrupted. "Pastor, you gave María medicine and now Casimero says she's pregnant. We want medicine so Marcela will have a baby too."

Some Bible School events caused more excitement than passing out medicine.

"Do you smell smoke?" I asked early one morning. Thatched roofs, the usual roofing on the *altiplano*, caused my fifth sense to work overtime when it came to smoke.

I jumped out of bed and peeked out the window.

"Oh, the Bible School kitchen is on fire," I yelled. "The straw roof is ablaze!"

We flung on clothes and Roscoe ran out to spray it with water but found the hose frozen. Someone had left it out all night. I ran down to get Cammack's hose, but it was broken. So the students formed a bucket brigade to carry water from the lake to douse the fire. Others climbed to the roof and threw burning straw off into the yard. Fortunately, oxygen is thin at 12,500 feet altitude and with no wind the fire burned only the kitchen and dining area.

"Guess what caused the fire," Roscoe said as we sat down to eat a breakfast of hot cereal and toast.

"A careless cook I suppose."

"No. Someone put the stovepipe up through that gunnysack ceiling and through two feet of straw without encasing it in cement or tile."

"Well, for land's sake," I mumbled through a mouthful of toast. "I'm surprised it didn't catch fire sooner. That cuts out our work for us before another year."

"Yes, we will need to replaster and paint, replace those gunnysack ceilings and build some more bunk beds."

"And wash the Bible School bedding," I added. "I hope some of the married women come early. It will be a job to wash 25 quilts. They can take it to the river, wash it, and spread it out on the grass to dry. Some will probably come back with holes rubbed in them, like some of your shirts did. Some smaller pieces may disappear if I'm not careful to count them. I hope the next shipment from the States brings some more quilts from the Women's Missionary Union. Some of these look rather tacky."

"They're probably better than what they have in their own homes," Roscoe commented as he finished his toast.

"Oh, lest I forget, the kitchen needs some *quinoa*. Eustaquia has promised to wash it this afternoon. I'll also need another gunnysack. She's decided it's easier and faster to put the wet quinoa in a gunnysack and tramp on it. I don't care how she does it, just so she washes the bitter taste out so the boys don't complain."

"In the storeroom last evening I noticed we're about out of meat." Roscoe pushed his chair back and prepared to leave. "I hope there's enough for today noon. The boys will butcher this afternoon. We're using about three sheep a week now, more meat than they eat in their own homes, I'm sure."

"When the cook knows there's plenty, she uses it," I commented. "By the way, I must remember to talk to her about cleaning the tripe better. Last week the boys complained that it hadn't been washed well. It had a bad taste and was gritty."

As the bell rang we hurried off to class, never dreaming that someday there would be 50 quilts to wash, much more *quinoa* to clean, and many more sheep to butcher.

For their room and board students worked for the farm or for the missionaries. They washed clothes, cleaned houses, butchered sheep, made adobes, harvested potatoes, drove the tractor, cleaned the warehouse, hoed the garden, or whatever needed to be done.

With only a few students that first year, we didn't need to buy much food. We killed sheep as we needed meat and used potatoes, *chuños, okas, habas,* and *quinoa* from the farm. However, we needed to buy some things at the store. In La Paz we bought flour and sugar in 100-pound sacks. For smaller quanities we shopped in Guaqui, on Saturdays. We loaded several empty flour sacks and at least two large bamboo baskets into the Jeep and drove seven miles to buy pasta, rice, *ají*, onions, garlic, *sultana* (coffee bean husks), cumin, oregano, and, in season, oranges. Ten kilos of pasta, 15 kilos of rice, a kilo each of *sultana*, cumin, and oregano, 100 oranges, and other food stuffs completed our purchases.

Salt arrived by llama caravan from salt flats beyond the mountains south of us. Each llama carried large blocks of salt strapped to its back. These blocks had to be ground on the grinding stone, a large curved stone that cooks rocked back and forth on a larger flat one.

We found it less expensive to bake bread for the students—*mariquetas*, hard French type rolls about five inches long. Every week two bakers appointed from the student body produced 620 delicious *mariquetas* from a hundred pound sack of flour, water, and yeast. They baked the bread in an oval adobe oven in our backyard.

After building a fire inside the oven with *tola*, Bolivian sagebrush, the students pushed the ashes to one side and slid in trays of little loaves. In a few minutes the hot smoky job produced fresh crusty bread, the staple for breakfast. With mariquetas and a hot sweetened drink (four teaspoons of sugar per cup) of ground toasted barley or toasted sultana, breakfast was complete.

Aymaras love soup. They served it twice a day in the Bible School dining hall. Simply made with or without meat but always with potatoes, *chunos*, onions, *ají*, and oregano, it's a favorite with everyone.

Since the potato is a native of the Andes, *chuños* and *tuntas*, dehydrated potatoes, were a staple in the Bible School diet. The process of making them developed centuries before dehydrated potatoes arrived on supermarket shelves in the United States. The method is simple and necessary for a people who have no refrigeration and must store potatoes from one season to another, or longer.

When the Aymaras harvest potatoes, they glean every potato, even those the size of marbles. They use these small ones, the wormy ones and maybe some the size of golf balls, if they have plenty, to make *chuños and tuntas.*

The method for making *chuños* is something like this: spread the potatoes out on a grassy area during the coldest months of the year, June and July, let them freeze at night, then mound them up in the daytime and cover them with straw so they don't thaw. Again on the second night spread them out under the stars. Mound them the second day to keep them from thawing. Spread them out a third night, but when the morning sun peeks over the horizon leave them in the sun to thaw. When the potatoes are completely thawed, the Aymaras take off their *abarcas* (rubber tire sandles) and tramp them with their bare feet, squeezing out the water and pushing off some of the peeling.

"What about the worms?" you ask. They're dead and add the needed protein to the diet.

"And *tuntas*?" They are made the same way except they are in water for at least two weeks, then frozen and dried. These are the Aymara's favorite.

When dried, the Aymaras pile *chuños and tuntas*, which can be kept for at least ten years, in a corner of the kitchen or in the darkness of a storeroom. The size of the pile determines a family's sense of security during drouth years.

"How do they use them?"

Soak them overnight then boil them as any other potato. People carry them to the field for lunch, cook them in soup, dice them in a scrambled egg. It's a versatile staple for the Aymara: finger food, the main ingredient for soup, and bread for breakfast if you can't afford bread or flour.

The Bible School cook added new flavors to the soup when we delivered wheelbarrow loads of cabbage, cauliflower, turnips, and carrots from the garden to the school kitchen. Here most of the students had their first taste of garden vegetables.

Good food, strong Bible teaching, encouragement, love, prayer, patience, and perseverance produced a healthy group of students with a love for the Lord. They fanned out across the *altiplano* to carry the Gospel to those who had never heard.

Students arrive for classes.

Peons tromping Chuños.

A cook grinds chili peppers.

6

PRAYER, PATIENCE, AND PERSEVERANCE

"*Señora,* Pascual's gone. He's gone," Braulio exclaimed frantically when Julia Pearson opened the door to his knock early one morning. "What do you mean, he's gone?"

"When I first awakened I noticed his bed was empty so I just thought he was...he was...washing his face and combing his hair at the faucet." Braulio slowly searched for Spanish words to explain the situation. "But his clothes are gone. And his Bible. He's taken his *bulto*...and left."

Calling the students together, Julia found that Pascual actually had left, leaving only the Bible School quilt folded on his bunk.

Seventeen years earlier Pascual Quispe was born on hacienda Suriquiña, a farm set at the foot of the snowcapped *cordillera*. Cold wind swept down from the glaciers, and frost permitted only a short growing season for potatoes, *quinoa*, barley, and *habas*. Snow occasionally fell in the winter months of June through August.

After his father's death three years later, Pascual's mother struggled for a living on this harsh, high plateau, the *altiplano*. The next year his mother sent four-year-old Pascual out to watch the sheep as they grazed on pockets of stunted grass and lichen higher up the slope.

Dressed in homespun pants and poncho, barefoot, but with a knitted wool *gorro* pulled over his ears, Pascual spent the day huddled behind a sod blind, a shield from the wind. Having gone to market with his mother where he had seen loaded trucks, he let his young imagination produce the perfect toy—a four-inch-long rock, which he ran between clumps of *jichu* grass. When he tired of playing "trucks," he imagined he played in the band at fiesta time and changed to playing the *quena*, a bamboo reed flute. Often Pascual peeked to see that the sheep still grazed close by. If they strayed far he ran after them, flinging a rock with his sling to corral them again. He watched carefully for small red foxes and Andean condors, which occasionally tried to carry off lambs.

As the sun's rays slanted long from the west Pascual gathered his *quena* and sling, then rounded up the sheep and started down the slope to his home, a one-room, thatched, adobe house, surrounded by a rock wall forming a patio and a corral for the animals. Here he crowded close to a *tola* fire in the smoky kitchen to thaw his chapped, blue legs and hands. As man of the house, he thrived on his mother's praises of "Well done, *papacito*" when he arrived home with all the animals each evening.

Pascual followed in the footsteps of his parents. Being animists, they worshiped Tatitu, the creator; achachilas, the gods of the hills; and Pachamama, the goddess of the earth. The mountains above them were sacred. Certain rocks had power. Spirits, both good and bad, lurked nearby, and fear ruled the Aymaras' lives.

When lightning struck near their house the people of the community tried to appease the god of lightning to ward off further strikes. Men pulled up their pant legs while women hitched their skirts above their knees, then all crawled around the rocky place where the lightning had struck, for this was now a sacred place.

The *patrón* did not think it important to provide education for children on the farm, so Pascual didn't go to school. But he had an analytical mind, always trying to reason why things worked the way they did.

As a teenager Pascual followed his loaded burro to La Paz at the end of harvest. After selling two sacks of potatoes and tethering his burro in the *tambo*, farmer's market, he wandered up Max Paredes street. Both men and women sat along the cobblestone street selling myriad things, some that Pascual had never imagined and others that spelled everyday life: oranges from the Yungas, bags of coca leaves and the bars of pressed ashes used in chewing the leaf, tiny boxes of matches, *anafes*, kerosene pressure stoves, five-gallon tins of alcohol, bags of confetti and serpentina, devils masks for the fiesta, piles of *ají*, heads of bananas, nails, wire, buttons, bars of Patria soap, and mounds of rubber tire *abarcas*, like he wore to town. Raising his eyes to an awning above, he noticed a rainbow of women's brightly colored skirts and embroidered shawls—fancy ones, not the homespun wool ones like his mother made.

To his surprise, across the street people crowded around someone explaining a picture. "Ah, that must be what Uncle Mariano told us about," he thought. Pascual's uncle lived at Uma Palca, below Mina Fabulosa. When he came down to La Paz, Mariano always attended church at Max Paredes, after his conversion through the efforts of believers at the mine.

Pascual entered the church out of curiosity, but came out a changed person for he too had given his heart to the Lord. When he returned home he started attending services at Chirapaca Friends.

Back home, however, he became restless. Herding sheep was boring. His mother remarried and soon his stepfather invited him to accompany him to Uma Palca.

"Mariano, this nephew of yours needs to be in school. He's 17 years old and can't read nor write. He's your responsibility." Leaving Pascual with his uncle, the stepfather went back over the mountains to herd sheep.

"Last week in La Paz," Uncle Mariano said, "the brethren at the church talked about a Bible School at Copajira. Would you like to go to school out there?"

Pascual's eyes sparkled as he nodded vigorously. When school started a few days later, he, with several other young fellows, got off a public truck and walked two miles to the farm compound. After enrolling he struggled, for he spoke almost no Spanish and could not do his assignments. Being quiet and fearful, he told no one of his problem, so soon became discouraged, thus prompting his disappearance from Bible School.

"Howard, get the car out," Julia ordered. "Pascual has gone. He's taken all his things and left. The others don't know when."

Howard sleepily got out of bed, dressed, backed the Chevy out of the garage, then honked the horn. Julia came running.

On the two-mile trip to the main road, Julia prayed. She prayed they would find Pascual. She prayed for discouraged students. She prayed for patience in teaching these slow ones. She prayed for physical strength to do what had to be done.

"There he is standing alongside the road," she almost shouted, as they came within sight of the main road. "Slow down."

"He's probably waiting for a truck," Howard added quietly.

Julia hopped out and soon convinced Pascual to come back to school. They rode home in silence, but Julia had already planned her strategy.

"Pascual, come across the patio to our rooms every evening," she explained. "I'll help you with your lessons."

He did. She did. And God answered her prayer.

Two years later Pascual's mother chose a wife for him, Nivesa, from a neighboring community.

"I'm going to be a preacher," he told Nivesa the first time he talked to her. "I'll preach the Word, I'll have no riches to give you, and you'll have no houses or lands."

"That's all right," Nivesa shyly answered. "I'll be happy if you are preaching the Word."

Martín Garnica, his pastor, married them at Chirapaca and Pascual and Nivesa returned to Copajira for his third year in Bible School.

After graduation they pastored on the *altiplano*, in the Yungas, and down in the Caranavi area. He served as president of the executive council of the national church two terms—one of those when Bolivian Friends became a Yearly Meeting. Later he and Nivesa served five years as missionaries in San Julián, a colonization project beyond Santa Cruz.

It isn't hard to imagine what would have happened to Pascual if the missionaries hadn't given him a second chance. Perhaps that bright smile, intelligent mind, and inquisitive nature might never have been used for the Lord.

Pascual is an example of several others who attended Helen Cammack Memorial Bible Training School because people in the States gave and prayed, because missionaries went the second mile, and because God gave fruit for our labors.

Pablo Mendoza is another product of God's faithfulness and of missionaries' prayers, patience, and perseverance. Pablo worked at a mine, high in the Andes. Miners may be tough but they can also be fearful. Being animists, they believe evil spirits lurk at every turn, and experience a certain apprehension at having to enter the mine, so protect themselves by offering sacrifices to the *achachilas* and El Tío, the gods of the mountain. Once a year the miners kill a llama or bull and splash the blood on the walls of the mine shafts.

Pablo knew about this ritual, for his father, Manuel, a tall, brusk Aymara, had carried on the same tradition when he built his house on the windswept *altiplano* near Pucarani. As a boy, Pablo watched his father kill a sheep and splash the blood on the side of the house, a sacrifice to Condor Mamani, the spirit of the home, to bring protection, prosperity, and blessing.

On a visit back home in Pucarani, Pablo found his father a changed man. Could his father, normally brusk and unpolished, show a more tender side?

"I'm going to town this morning...to meeting," Manuel mumbled, while eating a breakfast of boiled chuños and a cup of hot toasted barley tea. When he finished eating he went out into the patio, poured water from a clay jug into a chipped enamel cup, then rinsed his mouth. Chickens scattered as he spit the water where they scratched for the few grains left after his wife had washed the *quinoa*.

"Do you want to come along, Pablo?"

As both father and son, tall for Aymaras, strode along the path between clumps of *jichu* grass, Father told of finding the Lord and the change in his life. That day proved to be important for Pablo, for he too gave his heart to the Lord in the little church in Pucarani.

Back at the mine again Pablo soon became dissatisfied at the very thought of digging ore the rest of his life. He asked for his paycheck, walked back down the mountain and across the pampa to his home.

The first morning Pablo attended Sunday School the secretary wasn't present to call the roll. "Pablo, will you be our secretary this morning?" Tata Sirpa asked from the front of the room.

Proudly, Pablo strode to the pulpit, then opened the book to call the roll. With pencil in hand he looked out across the room, called a name, and made a check. Glancing again at the small group he called another name and made another check. One by one he called all the names, then closed the book. No one guessed that Pablo didn't know how to read or write. He had merely called the names of those seated in front of him, that he had known all his life. There were no absentees that day.

This experience humiliated Pablo, an extremely proud person, so he went home determined to learn to read. A few weeks later Pastor Sirpa announced the opening of Bible School at Copajira.

"I'm going to Bible School, Papá," Pablo announced to his father one morning.

"You don't need school. You need to take care of your animals and plant your land."

"I thought maybe you might take care of them for me," Pablo answered without thinking things through.

"Take care of them for you!" his father exploded. "I've got more than I can handle now. Take care of your own stuff." He stomped off, leaving Pablo to think about the situation.

Later that evening father and son ate supper while squatting by a smoky *tola* fire in their blackened kitchen. As they drank *chuño* soup from clay bowls and guided pieces of potatoes into their mouths with their fingers, Pablo tried to convince his father that God wanted him to go to Bible School.

"You didn't think I needed an education when I was small and now's my..."

"You still don't need an education," Manuel interrupted, cutting Pablo short. "What's reading and writing got to do with plowing and planting the land and guarding your sheep? I say it's a waste of time and I prohibit you leaving."

"I'm a grown man now, Papá. I was married three years to the wife you chose for me. She was a good wife but she died with that tumor on her neck, even after you took her to the witchdoctor." Pablo paused, then plunged on, "You can have my land, and you can have my animals. I'm going to Bible School."

A few days later a truck from La Paz stopped at kilometer seven near Copajira. Several young men, Pablo included, crawled over the side and dropped their *bultos* into the arms of another below. After shaking the dust from their ponchos and *gorros* they slung their packs on to their backs and started single file up the road to Copajira to Bible School.

Pablo had only one eye. Smallpox had taken the other when he was a small boy so he desperately needed glasses. The mission provided these and undoubtedly this one act of kindness caused him to develop a habitual beggarly attitude toward the mission. Nevertheless, being proud and stubborn, he plunged into his studies determined to learn.

"Pastor, I need to talk to you," Pablo addressed Roscoe when he opened the door one evening during Pablo's first year of study.

"What's on your mind, Pablo?"

"Pastor, I need your advice. I received this letter when Martín brought the mail from La Paz yesterday." He handed Roscoe a sheet of checked *carpeta* paper folded into an envelope.

"Well, it looks like your dad wants you to come home and get married," Roscoe said after laboring over the handwriting.

"Yes, and I don't want to go. He thinks I'll stay home but I'm going to finish school," Pablo nodded his head as though to punctuate his words. Then sheepishly he added, "This is the second letter I've gotten; I didn't answer the first one."

They prayed about it. We all prayed about it. Then one evening Pablo tapped on the kitchen window.

"Come in, Pablo," I called.

We sat to talk about the day's happenings. Finally, Pablo brought up the reason for his visit.

"Pastor, I've decided to go home and marry again. I know the Lord has called me to preach, and I know I will finish school. But I think God would have me marry Josefina. Will you marry us?"

"Sure, I'll marry you. Who is this Josefina?"

"I don't know. I've never met her. My dad chose her. She's from Patamanta. He said she's a hard worker. He also picked my first wife but she died of a tumor. I hope this one's all right."

The first week of vacation, on a Sunday morning, we drove to Pucarani. Excited believers filled the church for Sunday School and a wedding.

"Hermana, will you play the organ?" Pablo asked.

With that question I thought, "Why not make this look like an American wedding? The wedding party can march down the aisle while I play "Here Comes the Bride."

It didn't turn out quite like that, however. I dusted off the small portable pump organ and labored through "Beulah Land" and "What a Friend" while all sang lustily. As I launched into the wedding march, even though I pumped hard and fast, many notes stuck and some played out of tune so that wheezy rendition was barely recognizable. No one noticed, except me, for all eyes were on the wedding party as they came down the aisle, more in a group rather than one by one.

Our one-year-old, Beverly, didn't feel well that morning but she felt worse, abandoned, with her Mommie playing the organ and Daddy up front performing the wedding ceremony. All her brother, Gary, did for her didn't keep her from adding a few shrill notes to the service. She finally found comfort standing with Roscoe and playing peek-a-boo through his legs at the bride and groom.

Another little boy felt less intimidated. He picked his way around and over *mamas* who were seated on the floor close to the altar, then standing with mouth open, he stared up at this unusual service.

About halfway through the ceremony Manuel, Pablo's father, noticed a new couple arriving late for Sunday School. Leaving his place in the wedding party, he strode down the aisle to hold a lengthy, above-a-whisper conversation with the late arrivals. Then turning, he walked the entire width of the church, just behind the bridal party, grasped the collection basket and proceeded to take up their offering.

A few seconds later the ceremony was interrupted again when someone passed Roscoe a note. "After the wedding we will have a baby dedication," Roscoe announced, then proceeded with the wedding ceremony.

In a little adobe church, with straw covering a dirt floor, *mamas* sitting on the floor close to the platform, and babies crying and coughing, Pablo and Josefina promised to love and cherish until death parted them. From my point of view on the organ bench I could see through the window of the church to majestic, white-capped Mt. Huayna Potosí towering above the *altiplano*. Somehow it spoke of faithfulness, fidelity, standing firm through the storms of life.

The storms of life did buffet Pablo and Josefina. Back at Bible School the following year their little baby died of scarletina. I provided a white gown and blue blanket that Beverly had outgrown. Phyllis Cammack and Marie Chapman dressed him. We buried him in a newly made Protestant cemetery behind the church.

Aymara parents mourn the loss of their children. Being fatalists, however, they often said, "such is life" or "that's my destiny." With that attitude, Pablo soon plunged back into his studies.

Not all students at the Bible School finished the three-year course of study. Some left when they became homesick. Others from the lowlands couldn't stand the cold of the *altiplano*. Soldiers picked up one 16 year old student in Guaqui, forcing him to serve compulsory military training in the army. Some didn't like the discipline nor the afternoon work on the farm. We expelled two students because they got involved with girls, and sent two others home because they didn't want to obey school rules.

Of the 52 young men who graduated through the years, sad to say, some have not walked on with the Lord. A cult deceived one. Adultery claimed several. Divorce ruined one. Another left the church because the Mission wouldn't pay enough. But for the most part, the Bible School family worked, played, studied, and prayed together—a happy family. Today many graduates serve as leaders of the Bolivian Friends Church.

It took much prayer, however. "Come down this evening after supper," Paul invited. "Come for prayer meeting." We asked God for patience, wisdom, and guidance in settling both farm and Bible School problems.

Pablo and Eugenio came from the same community, Pucarani— enemies long before they arrived at school. From the beginning, Pablo, proud and aggressive, tangled with Eugenio, arrogant, a boss and hard to get along with. No one knows what caused their original problem, but they brought that baggage with them to school. They spent their time bad-mouthing and cutting down each other with sharp words, always trying to be number one. Their attitudes and actions were a bad influence on the other students.

One night the harassment got out of hand. At ten o'clock Paul and Roscoe had just gotten back from a 160 mile trip, a long day searching to buy alpacas.

"This is a good supper, but I'm too tired to enjoy it," Roscoe said as he finished his bowl of vegetable soup. Then we heard a tap on the window.

"Aren't you fellows supposed to be in your dorm at this hour?" I greeted them.

All three nodded, looking rather sheepish. "We have a problem. We need to talk to don Raúl."

"Pull up a chair."

They did and we talked.

"Pastor, Calixto and I are going home. Last night we had a fight in the dorm and Eugenio rubbed my ears until they're sore," Eusebio began.

I looked and his swollen ears looked as though they had been frostbitten.

"Cipriano shoved me off my top bunk in the scuffle, and I landed on my back. It really hurts," Calixto groaned to emphasize his pain.

"What's going on over there? Can't you fellows act like Christians?"

"The third-year students try to boss us around and call us names. We don't like it. We're going home."

Sensing the seriousness of the situation, even at that late hour, Roscoe called a meeting of both missionaries and students. "We're meeting in the chapel immediately for prayer," he announced.

Somber students and tired missionaries, eager to settle the problem, filed into the church to pray. Everyone prayed aloud at the same time for about ten minutes. Then one by one the students began to ask pardon. More tears and confession followed another prayer time. Pablo and Eugenio had threatened to leave but now they asked pardon also. At one o'clock in the morning we left the chapel, relieved to have won another battle.

Later that year another confrontation erupted as the students worked in the field one afternoon.

"You guys get to work!" A third-year student took off his belt and ran the second-year students through the belt line. At closing time they came back to the dorm—mad. The entire second-year class packed their clothes and planned to leave next morning. But Roscoe heard about the ruckus and again, took action.

On a crispy cold night the moon shone bright, and the Southern Cross hung low in the star-studded sky just above the willow tree, when Roscoe knocked at the Cammack door. Bingo, the dog, growled, refusing to recognize any other residents of the compound.

After discussing the situation Paul and Roscoe decided to have another prayer meeting. "It's eleven o'clock," Roscoe said as they strode across the compound. "They will be asleep but we'll awaken them."

A sleepy, tired, grumpy student body, still taking sides in the fight, were too mad to listen to either Paul or Roscoe.

"Let's go over to the chapel," Paul suggested. The men prepared for an all-night prayer meeting, if necessary. But it only lasted until 3:00 a.m., when most students felt they had settled their differences with one another and the Lord.

In addition to special prayer meetings to settle disputes, the school invited special speakers for spiritual emphasis week. Marshal Cavit, mission co-worker, preached several times, his favorite theme, holiness—santification. Most of the students sought the Lord with tears and many made restitution.

"I stole two sacks of *tuntas* when I worked for the farm before I accepted Jesus as Savior," Francisco confessed. "I also took some of the missionary kids' toys, a saw and a bit from the carpenter shop, 50 bolivianos, and a gunnysack." He wiped his nose and eyes. "I don't know how I can ever repay it."

Our hearts went out to Francisco, a *peón* boy. When he became interested in the Gospel, Carlos, his father, kicked him out and said he could not live at home anymore. Eager to learn, he fit in well, so the school became his home. After graduation Francisco and his wife, Asunta, went with us to open a new work in the Yungas. Then he suddenly died of typhoid, a valuable worker cut down at an early age.

Pablo also felt the Lord leading in making restitution.

"Don Marcial, when I worked at the mine several years ago I took some sacks and some nails. That's not very much but..."

"Pablo, it doesn't make any difference to the Lord whether it's a lot or a little, it's still stealing. You can never have victory until you make it right." Marshal put his arm around Pablo and they prayed. "I'm afraid to go to the mine. I can't pay it back and they might put me in jail." Pablo sought a way out without complete surrender.

"I'll go with you," Marshal encouraged him. Later, at the mine, they talked with the administrator.

"*Señor*," Pablo stammered to the man behind the desk, "several years ago when I worked here in the mine I took some nails and sacks. I know now that stealing is sin, and I've come to make things right."

"I...I...I really don't know how to handle such a confession," the administrator admitted. "I've never had anyone admit they stole things. You don't have to pay anything back. Just forget it." He reached across the desk to shake Pablo's hand.

The men walked out into the crisp mountain air. "It's a relief not to carry that guilt anymore." Pablo heaved a sigh and wiped the sweat from his forehead.

Through the years several students at the Bible School confessed to thievery, cheating, and lying. It's a way of life for those who don't know the Lord nor want to yield to Him.

"I don't want to be sanctified," Mateo said. "I'll be a Christian but I want to control my own life."

Felipe wanted to do as he pleased also. "Nobody's going to tell me what I can do."

One afternoon Roscoe prepared for a tent meeting. "Sorry, Felipe, but there is no room," he said as he tied down the tent on the trailer. "Some other time you can go." Five fellows plus tent meeting equipment piled into our Jeep for the three-hour trip to San Pedro Tana.

Other Bible School boys stood around to watch them leave but Felipe would not take "no" for an answer. Before the Jeep started to roll he dived in under the tent, wriggling to get comfortable on a wooden plank.

After what seemed like an eternity to one passenger, they unloaded their cargo in a courtyard in San Pedro Tana. Out tumbled Felipe, who had been bumped, beaten, pummeled, buffeted, banged, and whacked for three hours over terrible roads in a springless trailer! Some learned obedience quickly but Felipe insisted on doing his own "thing."

Young Aymara women didn't cause quite so much frustration. The first year of Bible School we had admitted four young women but only one finished the year. After boy-girl problems we decided we'd better not try any more coeducation. Even though Pearsons lived across the patio from the boy's dorm and the girls occupied a room next to the missionaries, they still had problems keeping track of the students. This problem pointed out the necessity of holding Bible School for the women during vacation months to prepare them to be good wives and co-workers with their husbands in the Lord's work.

For lack of space, missionaries limited the first classes to only two young women from each church. Eager to learn, seven walked 35 miles for the chance to study. The second year 45 arrived. The third year 54 came but 30 couldn't read. Finally, the attendance climbed to 75 young women.

As Phyllis Cammack described it: "Aymara girls and more Aymara girls! Fat girls, skinny girls, tall and short, pretty and ugly, smart and dull, well-dressed ones, others in rags, a few clean, others dirty, none educated; all with long black braids switching around, flashing brown eyes eager with anticipation; all with full, colorful skirts, bright shawls, and demure derby hats."

Oh, the excitement of learning Bible truths, memorizing Scripture, and learning about hygiene! They came with a purpose—to prepare to be good wives and mothers.

Each year some had health problems. One year mumps struck several. The flu visited often. One had an epileptic seizure. Apparently the *brujo* had put a curse on one girl. Paul had to revive her several times as we took her to La Paz to a doctor.

"I can't find anything wrong with her," the doctor said after an examination. "Evidently the witchdoctor has been at work."

Even health problems couldn't stifle the enthusiasm of these Aymara women. They found it difficult to leave when classes were over.

"It was a dark rainy morning when they were to leave," Phyllis wrote one year, "...28 of them to walk the seven miles to get a train, and 15 more to walk to their homes 15 miles distant. Four more had a 30 mile walk and a boat ride besides, to reach their homes. They did not want to go. They each shook the hand of their teachers, then embraced them; they had a little time of prayer together, sang `God Be With You,' shed a few tears, then started the process again, before they could be persuaded to start out across the brown fields and on to home."

As they left missionaries prayed they would be capable wives and mothers, future leaders for the Bolivian church.

Blood splashed on a home for blessing.

Aymara wedding

Cordillera beyond the altiplano.

7

STUDENTS IN ACTION

The Bible School curriculum required students to do practical training in Christian ministry. Mission launches carrying students and missionaries sailed Lake Titicaca to evangelize on islands and along the lakeshore. When fellow missionaries in La Paz borrowed the farm pickup for conferences, the students became accustomed to walking long distances to reach neighboring farms. Carrying portable record players and records from Gospel Recordings, Bible picture rolls, and a large poster entitled "Dos Caminos" (Two Ways), they set out two by two across the hills to spread the gospel story. Over the years these young evangelists started several new churches.

Needing transportation for students, we bought a Jeep from Monroe Perry, a Brethren missionary. He sold it to us when the government expelled him from the country for exposing the falseness of an image. With the addition of another vehicle at the farm, missionaries took students farther away to evangelize. News traveled fast and every year the number of students grew.

Carmelo Aspi, a government school teacher, walked several hours over the mountain to enroll in the Bible School.

"*Señor*, come visit my community," Carmelo pled shortly after his arrival. "We don't know anything about the Bible over there."

Such invitations thrilled us. Taking three students and Carmelo as guide, Roscoe bumped two and a half hours over a little-traveled trail to arrive at Parina Arriba. A leathery Aymara *tata*, wearing a black poncho, *abarcas*, and a colorful *gorro*, blew the *pututu*, made from a rams horn, to alert the community. Soon people arrived from all across the pampa to listen to their first gospel message.

Carmelo's attendance at Bible School opened a huge area to the Gospel on the back side of the mountain, the province of Jesús de Machaca. Years later Carmelo, his nephews, and cousins would become leaders in the Bolivian Friends Church.

For practical experience we felt the students should be involved with all church activities—conferences, three-day Quarterly Meetings and Yearly Meeting. The annual Yearly Meeting sessions always convened at Easter time.

The week before Easter government offices closed—business in general came to a standstill. Devout Catholics kept church ritual. On Friday they formed long processions through the streets to carry a casket containing a replica of a dead Christ and statues of the Virgin Mary. Many visualized Christ as dead from Friday night until Sunday morning so He couldn't see them when they broke the Ten Commandments. This belief forced the missionaries on Copajira to build a low thatched hut in each field of potatoes and barley where either *peons* or missionary boys could find shelter day or night as they guarded the crops.

Protestant believers also held special meetings Easter week to remember the death of Christ and celebrate His resurrection. In the early years from three to four hundred people from Friends churches across the *altiplano* crowded into the mother church in La Paz. They came to transact church business, to experience spiritual blessing, and to fellowship with other believers. They brought their blankets and at night people slept wall-to-wall on the floor of the church, and in the basement below. Some years a few overflowed to sleep on the mission porch.

When Bible School students presented a drama one year it became the highlight of Yearly Meeting. Phyllis Cammack, creative and artistic, wrote a drama about Daniel in the lions' den. The students performed to a packed house. Daniel, standing true to his convictions, was thrown into the den. The entire congregation of four hundred or more arose to get a better view. More agile fellows jumped up on benches for a glimpse of Daniel in the midst of a den strewn with bleached bones, lolling lions in their burlap-sack suits with sheep hide neck-ruffs and long trailing rope tails. Tears flowed throughout the audience as the cast sang "No, Never Alone."

Attendance at the annual Yearly Meeting sessions grew, partly because of evangelistic efforts of the Bible

School students. Soon the La Paz church could not hold the crowds. One year as the crowd marched by the altar to drop in their missionary offering, Jack Willcuts counted 1,100 people! "Four hundred sixty-five people on the outside couldn't get in," he reported. Practical missionary women thought of other inconveniences—only one water faucet and one toilet for such a crowd!

The next year nationals pitched a tent in the side patio, but even that did not remedy the overcrowded situation. Believers squeezed onto the platform, sat behind the altar rail, and filled the aisles. Some younger, more daring fellows either sat or stood on the windowsills.

Since music held a high priority for Yearly Meeting, missionaries cooperated on the pump organ and accordion. One year Roscoe added his trombone, much to the delight of everyone, for the trombone is not often heard in Bolivia.

Many sick people attended Yearly Meeting. They formed lines to get cough medicine, salve for impetigo, worm capsules, and Mejoral for a headache. Dust from the high plains and smoke from open fires in their kitchens brought patients for drops for red irritated eyes. Some came to have a tooth pulled—without anesthesia. Julia Pearson, Paul Cammack, Wilma Roberts and Roscoe served as official doctors in the mission. One year Roscoe prayed with every sick person.

"*Señor*,..." an Aymara *tata* whispered hoarsely. His little boy finished the sentence, "My father can't talk. He lost his voice five months ago. Please, he wants medicine," he pleaded. At a loss to know what to do, Roscoe gave him some cough drops, then prayed for him. The man, not a believer, went home where his voice gradually improved. Several weeks later he gave his heart to the Lord and testified to a touch from Him.

María testifies today to being healed when she asked for prayer. Some wanted prayer for their sick sheep or other animals. For the Aymara, God is interested in every facet of their lives.

Along with spiritual blessings and medicine for the sick at Yearly Meeting time, believers expected food three times a day. Country churches gathered potatoes, *chuños* and sheep for the conference. The mission provided transportation for the produce to La Paz. One year on the opening day of the conference Ralph Chapman made a trip to Pongon Huyo to pick up a load of potatoes.

"Don Raúl," someone informed Roscoe after service that evening, "we saw don Rodolfo fixing a tire out by Huarina this afternoon."

"Thanks, hermano. I'll go find him," Roscoe answered. Inwardly he groaned, *Oh, no! Ralph doesn't have a spare tire!*

Roscoe met him at the Alto. He had been fixing a back tire about every two hours all afternoon.

"Guess I have too much weight on this pickup," Ralph commented as he glanced up at the load of sacked potatoes with several believers sitting high on top.

"Yes," Roscoe nodded agreement. "With all that load the tire gets hot and melts the patches."

Feeding so many people taxed the facilities. Aymara women with brims turned down on their derby hats to shield them from the tropical sun, sat in clusters around shallow tin tubs peeling potatoes, chopping onions, and preparing *chuños*. One ground red chili pods and cumin on a rock while another cut jerky or fresh meat into small pieces. As the attendance grew from 400 to 2,000, so grew the number of 25 gallon drums of soup they prepared each day.

Excitement and blessing swept through the churches when fellow missionary Marshal Cavit built a tabernacle up on El Alto above La Paz as a memorial to his father. It provided room for 2,000 in services, more space for classes, a bigger kitchen and larger sleeping quarters.

The tabernacle also provided greater temptation for kids to sling rocks onto it's roof and more room for rock fights. Dust blew a gale across the tabernacle compound when a group of Aymara boys and two missionary boys playfully started throwing rocks at each other. When Gary Knight and Stuart Willcuts thought it time to quit, they turned to go inside. As they did so, a rock hit and cut a deep gash a scant half inch below Gary's eye, a fortunate miss.

That year Jack and Phyllis teamed up to produce a drama about the apostle Paul. The costuming with bathrobes, towel turbans, wooden swords covered with aluminum foil, paper helmets, and cardboard breastplates made a colorful production.

Nature provided sound effects when lightning cracked, thunder clapped, and it hailed hard about the time Iconium fanatics stoned Paul and Barnabas. The sounds of hail falling on a metal roof added to the dramatic effects and also left the audience feeling as though this was real live drama.

"*Mamas* moaned when Paul was beaten and left for dead," missionary Iverna Hibbs described it. "Men and children alike shed tears when Paul and Silas were thrown into prison. Babies cried, and many headed for the exits when a mock earthquake caused the tabernacle lights to go off and chairs and screens to topple. When cruel soldiers led Paul to his death, the audience fell to its knees. Many crowded around the altar to pray for help to live the Christian life." Such altar services were common at Yearly Meeting and brought renewed consecration and blessing to the church.

As the Bible School grew, so grew the problem of transportation. It wasn't easy to send 50 or more students to Yearly Meeting in La Paz. One year the economic conditions of Bolivia caused public transportation to dwindle to a trickle. Tires and spare parts could not be found. Fortunate to live close to Guaqui, we could board the train.

But returning to the school after Yearly Meeting presented another problem. "I could only buy tickets for the missionaries," Leland announced upon his arrival from the train station. "There is no more room for the students. Tickets are all sold out. Everybody is going by train since there are no trucks."

"I'll see what I can do," Jack offered. He was back in an hour or so.

"Any luck?" someone asked.

"You were right. They had no more tickets for 53 students so I rented a car on the train." He smiled faintly, waiting for our reaction.

"A whole car?" we asked in unison.

"Uh-huh, an entire car and it cost only 37,000 bolivianos."

The treasurer figured fast. "Less than 15 U.S. dollars to send 53 boys back to Copajira! Wow! That's cheap!"

For those living near Lake Titicaca a sailboat often provided a less expensive way to travel.

"Do you mean you really want to go to conference at Ojje?" Roscoe questioned me more seriously. "Don't forget, tomorrow is San Juan (John the Baptist), the coldest night of the year."

"Yes, I know but this will probably be the last chance I have for a sailboat ride across the lake. Why do we have to go at night?"

"Because the wind blows from this side of the lake at night." Roscoe hesitated then nodded. "Okay. Get the kids ready. It'll be cold. We'll leave the dock at six o'clock, just about dark."

This will be a fun trip, I thought. *True, many on land will be burning fires to warm San Juan's feet but we'll snuggle into sleeping bags and just hope it isn't stormy weather.* I remembered the times that other missionaries had crowded into *totora* (reeds) on the lee side of the island to wait out a storm.

I wasn't brave about water. Born on the plains of Kansas, miles from water, I felt fortunate to learn to swim in a mudhole. Lake Titicaca, 125 miles long by 75 miles wide, looked threatening to me.

Students, their wives and the Knight family boarded a sailboat at Guaqui on Friday evening to sail for Ojje conference. As we left, the sun dropped into calm water and only the oars made a ripple on the surface.

"I'm hungry," Gary announced while still in sight of the dock.

I wanted to enjoy the stillness of the evening but we ate our sandwiches, then Beverly complained, "I'm cold." So we crawled into our sleeping bags and joined the students in singing choruses.

The students curled up in their heavy ponchos and homespun blankets but lack of space kept some from stretching out. Twenty-seven of us in a 31 foot boat was a bit crowded for sleeping, forcing some to sit up all night.

"I want to go home," Beverly cried. Two-year-olds aren't thrilled with sailing at night. Gary thought it great fun until he couldn't stretch out to sleep.

Landing at 7:00 a.m., we found a skim of ice along the lakeshore and heavy frost across the fields. We felt the cold and understood why ancient Incas had worshiped the sun. We, too, longed to see it come over the hill. The pastor came to our rescue by inviting us to his house, where coffee and bread warmed us.

All agreed that the Ojje conference rated high on the success scale. Pastors taught classes, students held children's classes, Roscoe preached, I played the accordion, and the kids threw rocks into the lake. Blessings fell on one and all.

The students attended other conferences also where they had opportunity to teach and preach. Missionaries accompanied them to Amacari on a peninsula jutting out into Lake Titicaca, and to Chirapaca on the windswept *altiplano*.

One year Marshal and Roscoe took a load of students to Achachikala for conference. Along with a good report of meetings they gave a lively demonstration of how mice made a racetrack across their sleeping bags all night and how one got inside a sleeping bag.

Another time Roscoe and Paul took a group of students to Mina Fabulosa, high in the Andes. Roscoe's letter to the north is most graphic.

> On the way we had one flat tire, one blowout, with only one spare tire and no pump; so it was late when we arrived at the end of the road. There were riding and pack-mules waiting; so we rode to the top of the pass, crossed the glacier on foot, then walked down the other side. Some of the brethren were waiting for us at a division of the paths and were quite concerned that we were so late, as it was then night. They told us that the Conference would be at Uma Palca instead of the mine, so we walked (half ran) on down the valley in the moonlight for another hour and a half. We were well greeted, sang songs, ate a late supper, then because of the cold, Paul and I both crawled into one three-quarter-size bed instead of the two provided for us...
>
> Except for a few aching muscles, having the steering go bad on the pickup, leaving a student in La Paz by mistake, and not arriving home until 9:00 p.m., the trip was uneventful.

Another exciting conference took place at Copajira. On Friday, brethren from all across our field came by foot, truck, train, boat, or burro to attend the annual conference and graduation of Bible School students. One year 75 burros and 39 llamas welcomed us when we came out from the Yungas for the occasion.

"We fed breakfast to more than 600 people this morning," Paul greeted us.

Conferences, the highlight of the year for many, also served as training sessions for the Bible School students and pastors. One year, however, when there had been a critical spirit in the national church, we feared the Pastor's Conference would unite the troublemakers and lead to more dissatisfaction. Some came to complain against the mission, but several prayed until late at night and we saw the Lord bring peace and unity among the brethren.

Holding one two-week Pastor's Conference seemed like a good idea when we planned it, but a week of confrontation with the *peons* just before Conference left us wondering if we were wise to follow through with our plans. Tension had become so tight two soldiers came out to keep peace and guard missionary residences.

Where are we going to put everyone? I worried when a half dozen pastors arrived by truck from La Paz about noon on the first day. "We don't have enough bunkbeds, Roscoe," I complained.

"Jack said he'd be here with more equipment. Let's hope he can get through the mud."

I should not have worried for about dark Jack drove in with a load of straw mattresses, a tent, and seven pastors sitting high on top.

Pastor's Conference started that evening with only 13 pastors, but next day several more came across the lake from the peninsula. They used the school facilities but overflowed into the tent for sleeping purposes. No one minded the soldiers that stood guard. These conferences were essential in training pastors since as yet there were no graduates from the Bible School.

Students, especially graduates, anticipated the closing days of the school year. In the early years Roscoe took them to the Yungas for a three-day outing. But when the group grew to more than 50 students the staff confined it to a picnic, either in Desaguadero on the Peruvian border or down on the pampa on our own farm where the boys played soccer.

Along with fun times students and teachers also wrapped up the school year with more serious activities: exams, grading papers; an awards chapel; cleaning the classrooms, dormitory, and compound grounds; and celebrating with a banquet for the graduates—we called it a banquet for it seemed like one to the graduates and their wives.

The first class to graduate had only four graduates but as the years passed the number grew. To keep the banquet simple we served hotcakes and syrup. If the farm had killed a pig we added sausage gravy to the menu. But if not, the graduates relished bacon and eggs. Marie and I started the tradition but in later years Phyllis and Iverna joined the fun.

Most students had never used a fork so they learned to use tools of another culture. They also learned other interesting customs.

"How much syrup do I pour over a hotcake? My, how fast it pours!"

"Syrup with sausage gravy? We don't mix salt and sugar."

"Do I take a hotcake every time they are passed? Maybe so. I'll hold them under my shawl and take them home to Juanito."

The hotcake menu also varied with the weather. One winter it snowed in August so we made ice cream for dessert. Usually we served fruit and cookies.

The graduates received a Bible dictionary or a *Halley's Bible Handbook*, in addition to their framed diplomas to hang on their walls. One year the missionaries coming from La Paz forgot to bring the dictionaries. Roscoe made a flying trip to town. In his haste to get everything done, he framed the diplomas with the Bolivian flag upside down!

Pablo Mendoza, Braulio Espejo, Casimero Cuaquera, and Pedro Huanca were the first graduates from Helen Cammack Memorial Bible Training School. The exciting day arrived: graduates' diplomas and gifts waited in the office; Marshal and Catherine Cavit and Jack and Geraldine Willcuts arrived from La Paz for the celebration. Alas, we realized the graduates did not know how to dress properly for such a function.

Pablo appeared in red soccer pants and *abarcas*. Pedro wore coveralls that he usually wore in the shop. Braulio wore an old army shirt and blue soccer pants. Casimero alone dressed appropriately for the occasion.

"Are we pressing American culture onto these graduates?" someone asked.

"Maybe we should leave them as they are," Roscoe answered, "but they are setting a precedent today."

"Pablo, where's the suit doña Julia gave you last year?"

"I left it at home in Pucarani. I don't have anything else to wear."

We went to the storeroom. "Here's a pair of pants that will fit him...and a pair of shoes." Roscoe came out of the depths of a crate of used clothing that missionaries had brought from the States. "And here are four ties."

Roscoe tied the ties for the men and they walked out acting a bit embarrassed, but we thought secretly they felt proud.

After graduation Pedro went back to La Paz to work but the other three pastored churches. We thanked the Lord that we hadn't given up on them during a few challenging times.

Through the years 52 students graduated from Helen Cammack Memorial Bible Training School. Not all of the graduates turned out well but many went on to play an important part in the development of the Bolivian Friends Church—*INELA*. Later, Bolivians started their own Patmos Bible School and produced graduates. TEE, Theological Education by Extension, added more graduates. Some went to other denominations and others went into secular work, but from this group came the leaders of the Bolivian Friends Church today—missionaries, superintendents, evangelists, pastors, Sunday School teachers, school teachers, administrators, and faithful laymen. Helen Cammack would have been proud of them.

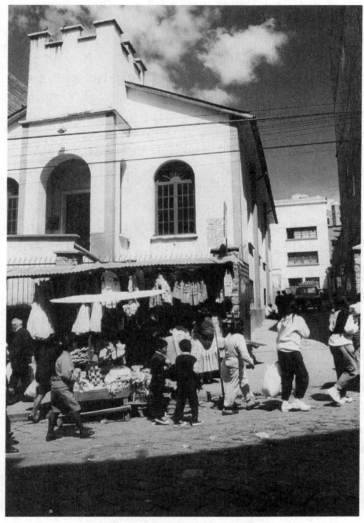

Max Paredes Church

Tabernacle

A soup kettle at a conference.

An Aymara lunch.

Evangelizing in a home.

A sail boat on Lake Titicaea.

8

MISSIONARY LIFE

Helen Cammack Memorial Bible Training School ended on a high note most years, but sometimes missionaries faced herculean tasks in both the Bible School and the farm. It seemed we met opposition at every turn and sometimes we became discouraged.

"If the pressure of problems doesn't let up I'm afraid we'll be one-term missionaries," Roscoe complained one evening after a trying day. "We need to keep our eyes on our reason for coming to Bolivia. It could be easy to lose our love for the people."

Weekly prayer meetings with fellow missionaries on the farm lifted our spirits. Each month we also met with missionaries from La Paz in council meetings to discuss business, report victories and defeats, pray, and fellowship together. These meetings, essential to keep the lines of communication open, encouraged us. Through it all God changed challenges into victories.

Mission policy required that missionaries spend one month a year at a lower altitude. Living at over 12,000 feet for long periods of time sometimes caused one to become extremely tired, irritable, impatient, and hard to get along with. When the pressure of the work became evident someone often said, "You need a vacation." Although we couldn't blame everything on the altitude, we knew that living in the high Andes left us with that "drained-out" and "letdown" feeling, an extreme fatigue that we'd never felt before living in Bolivia.

"Come go with us," we encouraged Jack and Geraldine Willcuts on our first vacation to Cochabamba. Jack had responsibilities he couldn't leave, for he served as pastor of the La Paz church, so he encouraged Gerry to take baby son, Stuart, and go with us in the Jeep. He would come down by train a day or two later.

We loaded everything that Gary and Stuart, our two babies, would need, then climbed out of La Paz and on south across the high plains. The rough dirt road wound by ancient *chulpas*, Quechua tombs for royalty of a bygone era, through villages of adobe huts with thatched roofs, and passed flocks of sheep where Aymara Indian *mamas* sat nearby, spinning wool into yarn while watching their sheep.

After spending the night in 14,000 foot Oruro, we jolted over a rough pass then dropped down from dry desert mountains to a green valley where eucalyptus trees lined lush alfalfa fields and vegetable plots. In this oasis Cochabamba, a Quechua town of red tile roofs, welcomed us.

Along dirt streets white flags marked corn *chicha* taverns. Women with white high-crown hats tended these local stills. In years gone by they sat around large clay pots, chewing corn to a paste, then spitting it into the pots where it fermented into *chicha*. To combat tuberculosis the government finally prohibited this practice so they now use other methods of fermentation.

Here in this warm valley we could take off our ever-present sweaters, eat ice cream (supposedly pure), and rejuvenate our strength, spirits, and frazzled nerves. Cochabamba! Perpetual spring! We longed to hear God's call to work in this wonderful climate.

"Two days to go 300 miles. What roads!" Roscoe stretched a bit before carrying our suitcases into the Bolivian Indian Mission home.

"What lovely warm weather!" A wail from the blanket Gerry held cut short her comment on the weather. Three-month-old Stuart let it be known the routine of eating could not be interrupted by weather forecasts.

Thus, we settled in for our first vacation in Cochabamba. When Jack arrived, he and Roscoe jumped on the motorbike to roam the town in search of a good tennis court.

"Hopefully someone down here will see the `For Sale' sign and offer to buy this bike," Roscoe explained. "Some fellow in Kansas gave it to me for the farm, but it doesn't have any power in the altitude. Since a motor loses 40 percent of its power in the altitude, I need a large motorcycle." They roared off for fun and business, all rolled into one.

A week later Roscoe wrote his folks, "It's been a fun week...just eating, sleeping, reading, walking, cycling, picnicking, swimming, playing tennis, playing games, and teaching Gary the word *luna* (moon)."

All good things must come to an end, so we packed to go back to La Paz. Up, up, up we climbed out of the

Cochabamba valley, leaving the green of the valley, the red tile roofs, the warm weather at 8,000 feet, and ice cream, as well as the wherewithal to heat a baby bottle.

"What shall I do?" Gerry worried when Stuart let his hunger pains be known but refused a cold bottle.

"It will only take a minute," Roscoe explained as he stopped in the top of the Andes. Crawling under the Jeep, he held a can to catch hot water from the radiator, forgetting it would be too hot to handle.

"Ouch! Oh, I've dropped the plug. All the water's running out!" He watched helplessly as the scalding water filled the can and drained onto the ground.

We looked at each other in disbelief then out across the top of the Andean range. "I wonder how far we are from water here?" Jack asked, not expecting an answer. Probably miles from any river or house. Not even a mudhole.

"Here, take the baby's water from the jug," Gerry offered as Stuart contentedly nursed his warm bottle.

"There's less than a quart," Roscoe calculated as he poured it into the radiator. "We'll go slow and hope it doesn't boil away."

We climbed up, then coasted down, up, down, up, down—slowly inching our way for several miles.

"Down there. See that grassy spot? There must be water," someone shouted.

"Where?" Roscoe slammed on the brakes.

"Down there about a quarter of a mile," Jack pointed off down the hill toward a green spot in the distance.

"Our next problem," Roscoe hesitated, "is what to carry water in. We only have that #2 tin can. That will be like carrying water in a thimble and will take forever."

Then an idea struck. "Oh, I know. My hat...just the thing." The fellows promptly hiked off down the mountain, over rocks, lichen, around clumps of sticky jichu grass, carrying an old pith helmet.

Puffing and panting, they carried enough water from the mudhole to meet the needs of the Jeep for the moment.

"Maybe it will get us to a river," Roscoe panted. "I'm not fond of climbing up and down these mountains at 15,000 feet—not much air up here."

"No, me either," Jack gasped, "but the view is beautiful—fluffy white clouds dotting a deep blue sky over folds of dark purple mountains. Gerry would enjoy painting this."

Counting our blessings, we drove on to La Paz, the end of an exciting and restful vacation. Now obstacles didn't seem quite so insurmountable. Even with a vacation each year, we looked forward to a furlough every four years.

We thought a furlough would be a vacation but quickly learned that furloughs are a change, but they're not very restful. Back in the Northwest we pulled our 18 foot travel trailer to every church in Oregon Yearly Meeting to tell the exciting story of Copajira and the Bible School.

The most exciting part of our furlough, however, was the arrival of another addition to our family, Beverly Joan, on a five-degree-above-zero day in Kansas, January 3, 1950.

Furlough soon came to an end and we boarded a 12 passenger Grace Line freighter in New Orleans to begin our trip "home." With Gary on a leash and Beverly in arms, we sailed to Arica, Chile, then took a train up to Bolivia. Back home on Copajira we plunged into the work of training young men in the Bible Training School.

Upon leaving the States Walter Lee, Mission Board president, admonished us—"Never get on the defensive." With this advice we resolved to be optimistic, to love the unlovable, and to look for the best in everyone. Although it turned out to be a tough assignment, this attitude helped to make missionary work more enjoyable.

Fellowship with fellow-missionaries lessened tension in the work. Missionaries played games sometimes, shot off firecrackers on July 4, made ice cream when it snowed, and celebrated Christmas and Thanksgiving together. The men and our children even found time to go hunting and fishing.

During a conference at Ojje, Roscoe and Gary shot *chocas*, edible mudhens, from Casimero's *balsa*, a reed boat. A trip to conference at Mina Fabulosa, high in the Andes, always provided a chance to go hunting. Carrying a 22mm rifle over a glacier at 16,500 foot altitude caused some to shake their heads but Roscoe and Ralph enjoyed the thrill of hunting. Condors, large enough to carry off a sheep, feasted on mules that had fallen off the trail. The fellows left them to their feast but shot eight *viscachas* and a *huallata*, an Andean snowgoose. The *viscacha*, a member of the chinchilla family, has a long tail and looks like a greyish-brown cross between rabbit and squirrel. It lives in holes between huge boulders and thwarts hunters by dropping out of sight at a moment's notice.

We seldom took a day off to do nothing, but usually combined hunting or fishing with work. On one such day I stayed at home to care for the Hibbs and Knight kids while Roscoe, Leland, and Iverna made the boat trip to Parquepujio, where four national evangelists planned to hold a tent meeting. The missionaries helped the evangelists raise the tent and get started in meetings, this being the first tent meeting they had ever held.

On the way home the missionaries fished. Roscoe caught a lake trout weighing eight pounds. He thought it large until he landed the next two, which weighed 15 and 16 pounds and measured 30 and 31 inches long. I spent the next day canning 15 pints of lovely pink salmon trout.

Changing roles and pace helped us relax. We enjoyed visiting primary schools. While spending one day at the Chirapaca school, we doctored the sick and pulled teeth. Twenty people had from one to four teeth pulled. They groaned and wailed but all did remarkably well considering they had no anesthesia.

We also gave immunizations for smallpox. Starting about mid-morning, we worked steadily until the sun dipped into Lake Titicaca. When we decided to quit because of lack of light, we had used all our cotton and turned used pieces inside-out to swab the last few arms.

Occasionally Roscoe took time off for recreation that had nothing to do with mission work. One time the Hibbs and Knight menfolk made a trip to the Island of the Sun, to fish and explore the ancient Aymara ruins.

Another trip didn't end quite so happily. "I must make a fast trip into Chusi, Roscoe. Come with me," Marshal Cavit invited him one day during school vacation.

On the second day of their walk over the Andes Roscoe became extremely ill and could go no farther. Marshal left him in a thatched home along the trail and went on to finish his business. Two days later he came back with a mule, loaded Roscoe and climbed the trail to the *altiplano*. After a week in the hospital in La Paz Roscoe recovered from hepatitis and soon returned to work.

When we arrived in Bolivia the mission owned one vehicle, a 1941 Chevy, given by a generous donor in the States. One vehicle, however, is not easily divided between two families living on opposite sides of town.

Since Roscoe's hobby was fixing up old cars, we bought our own. The first one, a yucky pea-green 1938 Plymouth, he painted light blue. When someone offered him $150 more than he paid for it, he sold it. Later he bought a dull grey 1939 Studebaker, which he painted maroon.

"*Buenas tardes, Señor.*" A stranger from off the street greeted Roscoe as we ate in the Beirut restaurant. "Does that maroon Studebaker outside belong to you?"

"Yes, it does."

"Would you sell it?" After a bit of dickering Roscoe sold car number two.

The Mission Board objected to missionaries being involved as car salesmen but they didn't object to our owning our own vehicles. In fact, when two vehicles couldn't be stretched between six couples a few years later, several bought their own. In the first 20 years we lived in Bolivia and Peru, in addition to our two city cars we owned two Jeeps (one we sold to Hibbses and when they immediately had engine trouble we had to refund money), an English Land Rover of ancient vintage with bad brakes, two new International Travelalls, and two Volkswagen combis.

Since dividing a pickup between La Paz and Copajira seemed impossible at times, we rejoiced when the Paul Cammack family arrived announcing they had shipped a new Jeep from the States. When it arrived at Arica, Chile, Roscoe went with Paul to pick it up at the dock. They found someone had stolen the top and a few other things; otherwise, it was in good condition.

While they waited for the proper papers to be processed they spent one night in a *pensión*, a rooming house. Paul got up in the middle of the night.

"What does 'diggery' mean?" he asked Roscoe as he crawled back into bed.

"'Diggery'? I don't know," Roscoe answered sleepily.

"Well, when I was coming back to the room I didn't remember which room it was," Paul explained, "so I opened a door and quietly called `Roscoe.' Some fellow said 'diggery.' I didn't understand so I backed out and finally found the right room."

By then Roscoe understood and sat up laughing.

"He said *'dígame.'* That means, 'tell me' or 'what?'"

They both went off to sleep chuckling over Paul's first Spanish lesson.

The next day, with no top on the Jeep, they climbed to the top of the Andes. Shivering in the icy wind and leaning as close to the windshield as possible, they jolted in and out of mudholes all day and all night in pouring rain. Arriving at the Bolivian border at early dawn, they waited two hours until the border patrol let them cross. An uncomfortable trip, however, proved to be a profitable one, especially for the Bible School, for it left a vehicle at the farm when we needed it.

Rainy weather and travel seemed to spell problems in Bolivia. One day as we waited for Jack's arrival for Pastors Conference, Roscoe and I reminisced about travel problems we'd encountered during rainy season while living at Copajira.

"Remember the week we pulled four trucks out of our river." I remarked, worried for fear Jack would get stuck in the mud. "When Pearsons went to town last month they couldn't get back with their car. It rained every day for a week, and the rivers ran full. Jack had to bring them out in the pickup, but he got stuck three times."

"Yes, I know, but everything will work out fine. Don't worry. This time, however, we're not going to sit up on the bluff with binoculars," Roscoe said. "He'll have to walk up to the house if he needs help. I hope he gets here before dark because we don't have the lights hooked up on the tractor if we have to pull him across the river."

"I'm getting tired of being awakened at night to pull someone across that river," I grumbled.

"I didn't go down the last time because I didn't have lights. That fellow wasn't very happy when I made him wait until daybreak, but I couldn't do otherwise. When I finally pulled him across he just drove off with only a slight nod of the head. No offer to pay. Not even a 'thanks.'"

"At least our own missionaries express appreciation for help. Remember when Howard brought the pickup out from La Paz and got stuck in the little river near Tiahuanacu? When you went to get it the soccer balls he had bought for the Bible School were floating around the steering wheel in the cab."

"Yeah, but my most vivid memory is having to completely overhaul that motor—full of water and sand."

"I don't think Howard had much love for that pickup, did he?"

"I'm sure he didn't. Jack loves to tell about their trip to Pucarani. Howard drove but he always had a hard time shifting gears. It seems he could never learn to double-clutch the thing.

"'We stopped along the road to pick up some brethren,' Jack's eyes twinkled as he told it, 'and when we started up again Howard couldn't get the thing in gear. He tried and tried. Finally, with his foot on the gas, he yanked it into gear. When it lurched forward, I looked out the back window to see four pairs of heels go over the tailgate. Fortunately, they all got up laughing and no one was hurt.'"

We had a good laugh remembering how Jack doubled with laughter when he told that story. "I wish we could tell more funny stories of travel on the *altiplano*," I said wistfully. "The first year we lived here at the farm we should have caught on that travel would have its problems. Remember when we spent the night in the pickup at the Tambillo bridge?"

"That was a foolish trip," Roscoe shook his head. "The Tránsito (police) fellow at Guaqui told me that we couldn't get through the rivers but I didn't listen to him."

"I have a feeling we should have listened more instead of trying to prove that we knew best."

"I suppose so but we tried. When we got to the Colorado River we asked a fellow to walk across the river for us so we could see how deep it was. He only showed it about two feet deep so I disconnected the fan belt and started across, but dropped into a hole. It took 45 minutes to dig out."

"Yes, but worse than that, I remember getting to the top of Tambillo hill and looking down over the river and valley and seeing only water. I was scared! I'm not as brave as you are."

"But we made it, even if we had to spend the night in the pickup. Thankfully, those fellows with their bulls came next morning about dawn. We just followed them across the bridge."

"What we should remember most about that trip was how God led us across that bridge and around a curve covered with water with deep drop-off's on both sides. I'm sure God protects more often than we realize."

Jack's arrival interrupted our conversation and we focused on Pastors Conference.

Copajira proved to be the ideal place for various functions of mission work. Along with Pastors Conference, and Bible Schools for both men and women, Copajira also hosted Aymara classes for missionaries.

After the Bible School closed in 1952, 15 missionaries plus some spouses and children from six denominations, and four national informants arrived for three months of intensive Aymara study. Since Cammacks were in the States on furlough, their house became dormitory, dining hall, and study hall for 30 people. Ellen Ross, from Wycliff Bible Translators, wrote the grammar and taught classes, which began at 8:00 a.m. Other than an hour off at noon and another hour for recreation from four to five p.m., students spent the rest of the time in grammar classes with Ellen, two hours of conversational Aymara with an informant, and in study.

Thanksgiving day provided a break in study when many missionaries from La Paz chartered the auto-carril, a rail bus, and came out to spend the day with us. Sixty-nine enjoyed roast chicken and all the trimmings. Lack of table space pushed us outdoors into a lovely day.

The men took another break from study one night when they all crowded into our living room to listen to the U.S. election returns on Voice of America over our shortwave Zenith radio. They finally drifted off across the compound at 3:15 a.m., happy that Dwight Eisenhower won the election for president.

Some students weren't linguists so dropped out of the classes. Roscoe studied hard and with an ear for languages he stayed in the top four of his class.

"How did you do on your test?" I asked one noon.

"Not so good," he replied. "I'm really not concerned about tests; I just want to learn to speak Aymara."

Aymara classes proved to be the springboard that launched Roscoe into speaking the language. Unafraid of making a mistake, he gladly accepted the help from believers, even in the midst of a message, when he lacked a word. Speaking the language of the people proved to be a big asset to the work. Aymara *mamas* and *tatas* beamed with pride when they heard their language being spoken by the missionary. It built rapport between national and missionary, and helped in dealing with the *peons* on Copajira.

A speaker has a big advantage when his message isn't processed through two interpreters—from English to Spanish and from Spanish to Aymara. Other missions realized this fact and asked Roscoe to speak at their Easter Conferences. One year Jimmy Lentz of World Gospel Mission spoke at our Easter conference.

Roscoe interpreted directly from English to Aymara with that same rapid-fire preaching that Jimmy used. No one slept and blessings fell.

We rejoiced to see the Aymara response but little did we realize that dark days lay ahead.

Balsa on Lake Titicaea

Medical work

Too deep to cross.

9

DARK DAYS

The year 1953 proved to be a year of frustration for all the Friends missionaries in Bolivia. Everyone adapted to unexpected and unpleasant situations. Without the Lord we would never have made it through that year.

Karen Faye, our third child, arrived on a rainy February Friday the thirteenth, making it the bright spot of the year for us. Roscoe plowed through mud and water to get to La Paz in time to welcome this new daughter into the world. Her entry was a stormy one, leaving me with debilitating health problems.

One month later I came down with hepatitis. Thankful for help from fellow missionaries, we left Gary and Beverly in Marie and Catherine's care, either in La Paz or at the farm, and Iverna cared for Karen, while I spent 21 days in the American Clinic. Ralph and Roscoe swapped work—Chapmans moved to the farm so Ralph could teach Bible School classes for Roscoe, while Roscoe attended to official mission business in La Paz to be near me. When I finally went back to the farm, though still too weak to teach, Catherine, Iverna, and Roscoe taught my classes. The Bible School experienced a complete fruitbasket upset.

Copajira also underwent changes. Mark and Wilma Roberts moved to the farm to help Leland with the work. Crops produced an abundant harvest—the biggest we'd ever had, so Mark ran the tractor and combine while Roscoe and Marshal taught school each morning then hauled potatoes and barley every afternoon. Leland supervised the entire operation.

All in all, with worry, health problems, farm tensions, and fatigue, a heavy work schedule took its toll on the health of all the missionaries. Both Mark and Leland came down with hepatitis. Marie's blood pressure soared, later forcing them to leave the field for a time. Leland's blood pressure and emotional condition caused the doctor great concern. Roscoe's two bouts with hepatitis required him to be on medication and diet for months.

Farm problems also tipped the stress level. During my time in the hospital people from Jesús de Machaca, a community on the back side of the mountain, cut a ditch across our land to mark a new boundary, taking about a thousand acres off Copajira.

Officials gathered in our front yard to discuss the situation. After drinking glass after glass of beer, their argument ended in a drunken mess. Authorities in both Guaqui and La Paz urged us to fight the case in court, but the missionary men refused.

"Since we are foreigners we can't gain by taking it to court," Roscoe explained to Leland. "It's better that we let them have the land, for the Machacans are a mean bunch who slaughter as they go if they can't have their way. They burned the roofs off several houses last week in another community. I'd rather keep peace with them, even though the judge thinks we're weak for not standing up for our rights. If we make enemies we'll always have trouble with them and never win them to the Lord." God honored this decision, for the Machacans never came back to claim the disputed land.

About this time the government proposed a new law, the Agrarian Reform, which would give all the big *haciendas* back to the *campesinos*, the country people. This caused great concern for the owners and provided the hottest topic on the gossip line. Since we had already offered our *peons* titles to their land, we thought we had nothing to worry about. Greedy campesinos, spurred on by an abundance of crooked lawyers, stirred the pot of discontent throughout the *altiplano*. We feared this climate would spawn a revolution.

The economic situation in Bolivia, that of hunger, inflation, and corruption, had often caused revolutions. Transportation stalled because of lack of gasoline. Stores closed for lack of merchandise. Fresh fruit and vegetable markets were empty. Staples, such as soap, sugar, and cooking oil, couldn't be found. Children stood in bread lines because of the scarcity of flour. Women, crying for bread, paraded with empty baskets on their arms in front of the president's palace. Their husbands, civilian men carrying guns, patrolled the streets under martial law.

Many an Aymara woman carefully folded her shawl to hide a precious cup of sugar, secreted to her because of her status as "favored customer," even though at first she had been told there was none. She also carried, hidden in her *bulto* and wrapped in newspaper, a half kilo of rice she had bought on the black market.

Costs of foodstuffs soared. The money exchange dropped. Each week Copajira opened its warehouse on Thursdays to sell potatoes, barley, *chuños*, and *quinoa* to hungry peasants.

Party politics also caused some revolutions. Crosses mark the edge of a narrow Yungas road where government officials were pushed to their deaths into a thousand-foot abyss. Even though soldiers guarded every street corner in La Paz, the *Diario* newspaper building, the Labor building and traffic offices went up in flames. Lucky government officials escaped across the border to Peru and Chile. Two leaders of the ruling party committed suicide.

Other revolutions ignited because of antiforeign feeling. *Time* magazine reported that the government of Bolivia wasn't capable of running its own government so should be divided among neighboring countries. This issue of *Time* didn't get into the post office boxes but they were stacked and burned in the U.S. Embassy yard.

Police searched the homes of six American families. A homemade bomb, lobbed over the high wrought-iron fence, exploded but did little damage in the American ambassador's yard. Rebels burned twenty cars and trucks belonging to the Point-4, a U.S. aid program, and formed demonstrations against American imperialism. Rebels targeted the American Clinic because it was American. They also burned Cruz del Sur, a Christian radio station. We left town without securing the required official permit but had to wait two hours at the traffic control while officials buried their dead.

Sometimes the opposition bombed targets across town so it didn't affect the mission. But at other times sandbags blocked our street corner and young fighters sighted down both Max Paredes and Santa Cruz streets.

One Sunday leaders dismissed services so believers could flee for home before fighting became intense. Another year a revolution cut short the annual Easter Conference.

On an island in Lake Titicaca *peons* burned the hacienda house and destroyed crops. Peasants marched on Cochabamba, fought in the streets, then stoned a missionary with a truckload of children.

Friends missionaries experienced tense times during one revolution. Gene and Betty Comfort, Ron and Carolyn Stansell, five kids, the maid and a dog spent a day and a night on the floor of their home while airplanes strafed the university, an army base and other targets nearby. Soldiers broke down their gate then entered the house without knocking. "We understand the CIA lives here—we see the antenna on the roof," one barked. Convinced that Gene didn't belong to the CIA, they then demanded the Volkswagen microbus. The missionaries never saw it again.

Revolutions, however, touched only a few believers. One year as Ralph and Marie prepared to leave for the States, they bade good-bye to various believers. After the usual words of encouragement and an *abrazo*, pastor Feliciano Sirpa, a veteran pastor, sent them on their way with these words ringing in their ears: "Don't you think the Lord is coming soon? Surely we'll see Him soon."

Chapmans recalled those words a few days later when they heard that Tata Sirpa had been killed by a ricocheting bullet as he hastened to his house high on the side of the city. Did he have a premonition that he would see his Lord soon?

Arturo Tito and son Javier have more frightening memories.

"Javier, your papa has been gone all day," Mama Gregoria said to her son. "Tomorrow morning you must look for him."

Javier, a boy of ten or eleven years, carefully searched every street and alley along the path his father usually took to and from his barber shop. Streets were deserted but friends peeked out when he knocked to ask about his father, then shook their heads and hastily closed the door and locked it. One knowledgeable person, however, suggested he go to the morgue. "A truck came by last evening picking up the dead," he added.

With heart beating fast, Javier turned his steps toward the morgue. "We carried a man next door that fits your description," a worker replied to Javier's question. "We thought he was dead but he moaned. Maybe you'll find him next door at the hospital." Entering with several other anxious ones, Javier waited to identify his dad then ran home with the good news, "Papa is alive!" Mama Gregoria, praising the Lord, nursed her husband back to health.

In the midst of troubled times God showed His care over missionary activity. While one revolution raged in La Paz, hoodlums, under the guise of rebels, broke windows and sacked stores and warehouses. At Copajira, Paul loaded a bountiful harvest of barley into a boxcar on the farm railroad siding to be taken to La Paz for sale. When the car remained there for several days he went to Guaqui to ask the reason why.

"*Señor* Cammack," the station master replied gravely, "had your barley been in La Paz, you wouldn't have anything to sell, for thieves would have broken into the boxcar and taken everything." We marvelled at God's protection.

Some months later, in spite of fears of a bloody battle, the Agrarian Reform went into effect on August 2, 1953, with few repercussions.

"Today all Bolivian *peons* are free," I wrote folks in the north. "Some landowners lost thousands of acres and 200 or more *peons*, the equivalent of much manpower or machinery. The Lord certainly led us when we bought Copajira—just 30 *peons*. We haven't heard yet how our land will be affected but we probably won't lose it because we've already given the *peons* titles to their own parcels, and Copajira is a high producer. The government likes that."

With tensions high, problems on every hand, my lacking strength to carry my end of the load, and Roscoe having continual health problems, we felt relieved but surprised when the Mission Board asked us to come back to the States for a rest.

We packed smaller housekeeping items but sold the Jeep, motorcycle, tools, guns, my Fostoria dishes—things we wouldn't need if we came back.

"It is hard to part with my Fostoria—a wedding gift," I confided to Janet Armstrong, who bought it. "But if we're going to be missionaries all our lives, I don't need it."

"We still feel perfectly clear about coming home," we wrote to family in the States. "We believe we are definitely in the Lord's will. Making a decision when we aren't well physically has not been easy but we don't think we'll be coming back to Bolivia unless God makes it clear. We trust in Him and have no fears."

Always wanting to see new country when we traveled to and from Bolivia, we flew off to Argentina to visit college friends, on to Uruguay to spend fun days with missionary friends in Montevideo, then on north through Brazil.

We appreciated Lloyd Aereo airlines giving eight-month-old Karen free baggage allowance when we left La Paz, even though they didn't charge airfare for her. Argentinian and Uruguayan Airlines did the same. But when we checked in at the Brazilian Airline office in Río de Janeiro, they weren't so generous. In fact, they charged airfare for Karen plus $60 excess baggage.

After checking in and waiting for our departure, the intercom paged Roscoe.

"We have a gentleman who needs to make this flight. Would you be willing to make room for him by holding one of your two older children on your lap?" the man at the ticket counter asked.

Immediately Roscoe thought of the unjust charges he had just paid and the prospect of having to hold two children on a long overnight flight over the jungle.

"No. I'm sorry, but that wouldn't be comfortable for such a long flight."

A short time later we boarded a packed plane. We took off, then instead of flying the flight pattern and heading northwest across the Amazon jungle, the pilot kept circling above the city.

"*Señor*," Roscoe asked the steward, "is there a problem? We've been up several minutes but haven't gained altitude and just keep going in circles."

"We have too much weight and can't gain enough altitude to get over the mountains," the steward replied. "No problem, no problem. We'll just change course and fly the coastline. We'll refuel at Recife."

As the steward went on down the aisle, our eyes met knowingly. *Evidently the "gentleman" got on board with all his baggage.*

Along with an overload of passengers and freight, a vibration in the tail section of the plane kept us uneasy so we rejoiced to fly the coast instead of across the Amazon jungle.

As we landed in Carácas, Venezuela, 25 hours later, a voice over the intercom brought welcome news.

"Sorry for the inconvenience but this plane needs some repairs. We'll be here overnight."

The next morning at 4:30 we gathered in the lobby, awaiting our ride to the airport. Three extremely tired Knight kids sat quietly side by side on a leather sofa.

"Lady," a sleepy-eyed, unshaven passenger addressed me, "You don't have children, you have angels."

I agreed. Looking at them, I wondered, "Do angels get tired?" Maybe so, but these angels were as good as gold—perfect travelers!

Six hours later as we went through customs in Miami, Roscoe passed the steward of our plane.

"Thanks for a good trip," Roscoe said. "Are you heading back to Río tomorrow?"

"No, we'll be here for a few weeks. Our plane has to have a complete overhaul."

Again our eyes met over the heads of our children. We understood, for we felt the Lord's arms under us with every vibration, lifting that extra overload, and taking care of the broken gas line and oil slick.

After a leisurely trip across the United States, visiting family along the way, we pulled a 28 foot house trailer into the desert at Twenty Nine Palms, California, to spend the winter.

With the solitude of the desert, rest, and warm weather, we slowly regained our physical strength. But better yet, we dug deep into God's Word and felt Him lay missions upon our hearts again. God's call took us back to Bolivia to plant churches in the Yungas on the eastern slopes of the Andes mountains.

Knight family—1953

10

PERSECUTION

Planting churches in Bolivia in an unevangelized area often provoked persecution. In the late 1920's when Friends first started work in Bolivia, Juan Ayllón started a small church in Chicharro, around the tip of the peninsula, a rocky promontory jutting out into Lake Titicaca.

"Stay," someone begged at the close of service one Sunday afternoon. "Stay with us and teach us. We are like animals." So Juan left three zealous believers from La Paz to teach this small group of new Christians.

Not everyone in Chicharro, however, accepted this new Gospel. Rumors spread.

"They pray to their god that it won't rain."

"Yes, and I hear they are threatening to destroy our church and burn the cross."

"I heard they plan to overthrow the government," a third added to the list.

The rumors inflamed a mob who descended on Chicharro intending to beat believers and burn their homes, but Juan arrived unexpectedly from La Paz. In their rage the mob turned to beat and kick Juan, then seized him along with five believers, and marched them off across the hills to accuse them before government authorities in Tiquina.

In spite of persecution new Christians witnessed to their neighbors, the church grew, and soon another small group started services in Amacari, a nearby community. Here, the Yucra brothers, Báltazar, Gregorio, and Francisco, listened to the gospel message but had doubts. They, along with friends, Pedro Huarina and Cruz Chipana, loved their fiestas but somehow felt this new religion wouldn't approve their dancing and drinking. Deep in their hearts, however, they wanted to accept Jesus as Savior.

"I've got an idea," Báltazar Yucra said to his brothers. "At the next fiesta let's dance the *challpani* but we won't drink. That will be our last fiesta."

Not everyone was thrilled with the idea. "You mean we'll give away our beautiful feather headdresses?" Báltazar nodded.

To the astonishment of their neighbors these new Christians donned their colorful headdresses, then formed a circle, and danced the *challpani* for the last time—without touching a drop of alcohol.

Cipriano Mamani and his wife, Petrona, came from La Paz to pastor these new churches on the peninsula. To reach the area, they had to cross the Straits of Tiquina, a deep, narrow stretch of water about three quarters of a mile wide. Vehicles loaded onto flat-bottom sailboats. With a good breeze, they sailed across to the other side. On a calm day or one with contrary winds strong Aymara men rowed the boat across.

Our first year in Bolivia the mission council had named Roscoe director of schools. With almost no public schools in the country areas, missionaries started one in Amacari. Many parents could not read or write. When they became converted they longed to read their Bibles and hymn books. They also wanted an education for their children.

Market days and fiestas provided opportunities for Christian school students and teachers to conduct street meetings, since people came from miles around to buy and sell. On one such day the believers in Amacari felt the results of religious persecution.

"Sing loud so people can hear," Pedro Quispe, Amacari school teacher instructed his students who helped conduct a street meeting on the corner of the plaza in Tiquina. Strains of "What a Friend" echoed across the town square.

A burro loaded with onions, their green tops bobbing merrily with every step, clip-clopped along the cobblestone street to unload at an empty space among other vendors. Aymara *mamas* sat behind piles of *chuños*, miniature potatoes the size of golf balls, and *okas* and *isaña*, tubers of the potato family. Others sold cartwheels of sheep cheese imprinted by woven grass molds, and fish from the lake—tiny minnows and larger bony bogas. One merchant offered purple five-gallon tins of alcohol, wine-size bottles of kerosene, candles and tiny boxes of matches, all of which he had brought from La Paz.

Now and then, while Aymara boys planted their feet against rocks on shore and held anchor ropes taut, a truck roared off a ferry and up the road, leaving dust to settle over the market.

In such confusion and noise Pedro urged his students to sing louder and he preached the message of salvation to all who stopped to listen. *Tatas* with wide-brimmed hats and homespun pants and ponchos; *mamas*, most with babies on their backs, in derby hats, bright shawls, and many homespun skirts; boys in colorful knit caps pulled over their ears; and timid girls, replicas of their mothers, all stopped to listen. They didn't linger long, for even though they might have been interested, they feared to admit it. Many in the village strongly opposed Protestants.

"What do you think of the virgin of Copacabana and the saints?" one young fellow called after stopping to listen.

Pedro explained what the Bible taught about worshiping idols and saints. The young fellow melted into the crowd.

Soon a portly village official strode up to Pedro. "So you will preach against our saints, eh?" With his doubled fist, he socked Pedro in the eye, knocked him to the ground, then continued kicking him, rolling him as though he were a football.

Afraid, students and believers ran. After several minutes Pedro regained consciousness and crawled into a nearby patio, where he lay until almost dark. Only when the vendors left did the students dare to search for their teacher. Finding him, the boys hoisted him onto a burro and followed the dusty trail up over the hills and down into the Amacari valley.

Word of all this activity reached us at Copajira the next morning. Within two hours Roscoe left for La Paz, then on to Amacari, where he discovered and brought back to the doctor a severely bruised and battered teacher. Pedro had not been afraid to declare what he thought to be truth of Scripture, but he suffered for his courage.

Pedro was not the first to suffer for his Lord in the Amacari area. Pastor Cipriano had become a beloved pastor who walked miles with his wife, Petrona, to visit and encourage his parishioners. Those who opposed the evangelicals, however, stoned him, burned the straw roof off his house, and scorned him when he refused to participate in community fiestas. They laughed at him when he took a dip in the icy waters of Lake Titicaca to cure himself of a fever instead of going to the witch doctor. Cipriano knew all about persecution, and he encouraged believers to stand strong in the face of it.

About a year after Pedro's beating, a telegram arrived at the mission house in La Paz announcing our loss. "Pastor Cipriano Mamani died this afternoon."

Jack answered with another telegram: "Missionaries are coming."

When word arrived at the farm next morning Roscoe took the pickup with Howard, Julia, and several students on that long trip to Amacari. But Jack's telegram didn't arrive until after the funeral. So as the missionaries came down the hill into the valley by the lakeshore, believers were shoveling dirt onto Cipriano's grave.

"He was sick only two days," someone explained. "He didn't want any medicine. He said if the Lord wanted him to live, He would heal him as He had done so many times before."

"Just before he died," someone else continued the story, "Pastor Cipriano said, `The missionaries didn't get here, but that's all right. I'm going to see my Lord and won't need them anymore.'"

The congregation gathered in the church another time for more encouraging words from the missionaries, then accepted Pedro, their teacher, as their pastor. Pedro, although much younger, already knew about persecution so would understand and encourage them in dark days ahead.

Copajira also faced persecution. Evangelism ranked high on the list of priorities for Bible School students every year. With portable phonographs and gospel records they visited every *peón* home on the farm, which resulted in several peons becoming interested in the Gospel.

Pedro Aguilar lived across the river—on the wrong side of the tracks, so to speak. He didn't run with the "in" crowd of *peons*, was bashful and timid but always had a smile.

Paul appointed Pedro the keeper of the pigs, which meant he carried the keys to the compound gates and also a key to the hammer mill where he ground pig feed. Knowing that honesty was a rare quality among the peons, Paul watched him closely.

On a sunny but chilly July day Bible School boys spread *tuntas*, dehydrated potatoes, on the grass in front of the church to dry. Pedro finished feeding the pigs then walked through the compound on his way home. Noticing the white *tuntas* bleaching in the sun, he stopped, picked up a handful—three or four—and walked on down the road.

Paul happened to notice so followed him down to the gatehouse.

"Pedro, I noticed you picked up a handful of *tuntas*."

"Oh, but I didn't take many."

"I know, but regardless of how many you take, that is stealing. Would you steal three or four sheep or three or four pigs? It's not the amount I'm thinking about. I just want to know I can trust you."

David and Daniel, Cammack boys, became good friends of Pedro and often on a Sunday afternoon a circle of fellows, including Pedro, lay on the grass in front of the church to discuss spiritual truths. We don't know when Pedro accepted the Lord but little by little he grew in his faith and became a trusted helper on the farm. Because of his honesty, he later worked in the Bible School kitchen and faithfully attended services at the church.

Four of the boldest, anti-Protestant *peons*, however, kept the other *peons* fearful of attending services.

"*Señor Raúl*, our family would like to come to meeting but we're afraid."

"There's nothing to be afraid of," Roscoe encouraged Luís.

"Oh, but you see, those four fellows say they will beat anyone who comes to meeting."

Two months later they proved true to their threat by breaking into Pedro's house one night, stoning him, hitting him on the head and chest. The next day, Sunday, only students attended service. Others were afraid.

About this time the Vatican published statistics that shocked the church—only ten percent of the Bolivian population were practicing Catholics. The Protestant church, though suffering at times, began to grow, so naturally the state church did everything to stop that growth.

"Do you know who is causing all the trouble?" the sheriff in Guaqui asked Roscoe one day when he sought help in solving farm problems.

"I suppose it's the *peons*," Roscoe answered.

"No, it's someone outside Copajira, someone in Guaqui who has a lot of influence." The sheriff stamped the document, and handed it to Roscoe. "I warn you against doing anything to antagonize the *peons*; it could cause serious repercussions."

We tried not to worry about the warning but *El Diario*, the La Paz daily newspaper, often carried stories about Protestant persecution. After the conversion of Walter Montaño, a Catholic priest, his hometown, Cochabamba, strongly resisted the Gospel. The Baptists tried to have street meetings but hecklers showered them with tomatoes and manure. Troublemakers also stoned believers in Sucre and Potosí.

Missionary Monroe Perry from Uyuni stood trial, accused of destroying an image. The truth was that he took pictures of believers taking an image apart to prove that it was fake, that it didn't have blood, that it was only plaster of Paris.

Posters, pasted on walls throughout downtown La Paz, aroused so much anti-Protestant feeling that even though missionaries pled with the president for leniency, the authorities ordered Perry to leave the country. Mobs formed to march through town, threw rocks through the windows of the Lutheran chapel, and stoned missionary Smith's car. On the *altiplano*, a drunken mob stoned believers and Baptist missionary Norman

Dabbs, to death. Seminary authorities forced student René Bardales, to stand outside in the rain for several hours one night because he visited an evangelical service. They also forced him to lie across the threshold where other students had to step on him as they entered. After conversion, he hid to keep from the wrath of his teachers. Likewise, José Rico, a young Bolivian priest, secretly visited Samuel and Gladys Smith to learn more about the Gospel. Later, after their conversions, both René and José became evangelists.

Even children experienced persecution sometimes. About 1940, missionary Helen Cammack held children's classes in her home on the plaza at Puerto Perez, a fishing port on Lake Titicaca. After telling a story about Jesus, she often gave the children cookies. Cookies, almost unknown to the country Aymara, enticed one little boy, Cipriano Copa, and he gave his heart to Jesus. Cipriano stood staunch against the taunts of his friends who tried to drown him in the lake because he refused to drink during a fiesta. Back in his home community of Karhuisa, he witnessed to his family and soon they too became believers.

Sometime later Pablo Mendoza and Julio Choque, graduates from Copajira Bible School, set up a tent for special meetings in Karhuisa. Karhuisa, a community scattered over folds of rocky outcroppings at the foot of the Cordillera, was influenced by anti-Protestants from Peñas, a neighboring community.

"Let's untie all the ropes," an opposition leader suggested. The tent fell but the young evangelists tirelessly raised it the second time for meetings that night.

The next day a group of twenty men vented their anger again with a hail of stones, then marched Pablo and Julio off to a provisional jail. The two young evangelists sat in a dark room all day wondering if their efforts to evangelize had failed. While praying and singing hymns, undoubtedly they felt a little like Paul and Silas.

"I think it's getting darker outside," Pablo observed, as he squinted through a crack in the door. "I wish we could have meeting again tonight."

"I don't hear anyone," Julio commented. "The sheriff spoke with someone outside the door a few minutes ago. Do you suppose they've gone?"

Cautiously, he pulled the door open. Squeeeek! They held their breath but heard nothing. Becoming braver, Pablo poked his head out to scan the patio. Empty! All was quiet.

"Come on," he whispered, "let's go. They're gone. We'll go have meeting."

They ran. Those who listened to their message that night marveled to see them free again. Fearless, Pablo and Julio didn't waver the next day when an angry mob threatened them with knives and clubs. They sang and preached for four nights. God added new believers to the church, a great encouragement to the small group of Christians in Karhuisa.

"It sounds like another chapter from the book of Acts," the missionaries commented when they heard Pablo's story.

Bolivian Christians suffered the most persecution, but occasionally the enemy aimed at missionaries, also.

In 1956, while planting churches in the Yungas, Roscoe needed repairs for the Travelall. Upon arriving in La Paz, however, he found all businesses closed because of a fiesta.

"Come with me to move the tent," Jack invited. "After we pick it up at Chuñavi, we'll take it to Puerto Perez, put it on a boat, and send it on to Calata for more meetings."

"I'd like to," Roscoe quickly responded. "We'll have time to visit as we travel."

"We won't get home very early, for I've promised to stop at Karhuisa for meeting," Jack explained. "They have church problems that must be settled."

It was almost dark when Roscoe, Jack, and his son, Stuart, turned off the main road to follow a trail past red sandstone bluffs, up into a narrow valley where believers met in a small adobe church with thatched roof and dirt floor.

Along the way a teacher from a Friends school nearby stopped them. "Pastor, the community people have been meeting in the schoolhouse all day. Someone said the priest from Peñas offered a short-wave radio if they would kill the Protestant evangelists and missionaries and burn their pickup."

"Thanks for telling us." The fellows drove on with a sharp eye for any attackers but felt rumors floated in the air that night. As they passed the schoolhouse they saw no light nor sign of activity. "Evidently everyone has gone home," Jack commented.

Arriving at the church, they found 40 brethren gathered for meeting. After the usual greetings they sang and prayed. Roscoe spoke for a few minutes but was soon interrupted when the door burst open.

"There's a mob down by the school," a couple of men announced breathlessly. "They have guns and dynamite and are calling for more." That announcement promptly broke up the meeting.

"They're yelling and blowing a *pututu* (cow's horn) to call all the people. They're carrying clubs, dynamite, picks, shovels, and rocks. Everyone's drunk."

Everyone's drunk! Those words struck fear to the missionaries' hearts, for they knew that they could not deal with a drunken mob.

"How do we get out of here," Roscoe asked. Everyone had an opinion as to what they should do. "You can't get out of here. There's only one road in and they have that blocked."

"Hide the pickup."

"Cover it with hay so it looks like a haystack."

"Hide in that little room with no windows so they can't see the light."

"They've cut deep ditches across the road and put big boulders on each side so you can't get by," announced someone who, under cover of darkness, had gone down to see what was happening.

"Can we go up over the hill?" Jack asked.

"No, no! That's all fields. They have guards with guns posted on the hills."

The sounds of yodeling war whoops, mournful calls from a *pututu*, shouts, and yelling echoing across the still night air sent shivers of terror through the missionaries. To make matters more unnerving, Aymara *mamas*, assuming they would all be murdered, gathered in the church, where their prayers, wails, and weeping at the top of their voices added to the sounds of the night.

After backing the pickup into a patio surrounded by an adobe wall, Jack and Roscoe followed a few men into the little thatched hut for prayer. Then they weighed their chances of escape.

"Don't worry. I don't think the mob will come any closer," one optimistic young fellow tried to encourage them.

"I'm not so sure." An older believer shook his head to discourage any rash advice.

"We can hold that one small door against the mob," Roscoe assessed. "But what about the roof in case of fire?" Both missionaries glanced up at rows of straw thatch laid on eucalyptus poles.

All stood quiet for several minutes. Only the sounds of the mob below disturbed their thoughts. Jack glanced at his sleeping son and wondered if he could make it if they had to run for it.

"There's a little-used trail up over the hill behind here," Mariano, their host, mentioned. "I don't think you can get over the gulch, but..."

"We'll try it," both Jack and Roscoe said at once.

"The bank is steep; we'll need to dig it down and..." Immediately Mariano went to find pick and shovel then sent two men up to level the bank a bit.

After what seemed like hours they returned announcing they thought the pickup could cross the gulch.

"*Bueno*. Good. Let's go."

"You can't go yet," Mariano objected, "you have to eat supper first."

Eat! That was the last thing the missionaries wanted to do! Courtesy dictated that they eat, so they gobbled the eggs, stuffed chuños into their pockets—ready to go.

Sound indicated that the mob was moving closer as the mission pickup eased out of the patio. Surrounded by about twenty believers with clubs, picks, and shovels who guided Roscoe out across the fields, around gulches, rock walls, and piles of rocks, they crept up, up, up, through the night.

"Don't turn on your lights," a believer cautioned, as he walked in front, lighting the way with a tiny kerosene hurricane lamp made from an evaporated milk can. Arriving at the gulch, with the pickup in four-wheel drive, they barely clawed their way over the top.

"Let's turn on the lights and get out of here," Roscoe yelled at Jack who was walking beside the pickup.

"No, no! Not yet," Mariano warned. "They have guards with guns on the hills above."

Shortly afterwards, however, throwing caution to the wind, they turned on their lights. Believers jumped into the pickup as they bounced across the fields, dodging rock piles and walls.

Arriving at a junction of two trails, someone pounded on the cab. "This way," he shouted.

"No, that leads you back to the mob," someone else hollered. "Go that way."

Not knowing which advice to take, they trusted the Lord and good common sense to guide them to the main road.

The next day they learned the sequel to their escape. The mob arrived at the church and Mariano's house. They searched everywhere.

"Where's that pickup?" they demanded. "Those *gringos* can't have escaped."

When believers refused to answer, they beat Mariano severely then set fire to his thatched roof.

Thirty-five years later Roscoe and I joined seven or eight hundred Aymara believers at a conference in that same community of Karhuisa. After Roscoe preached, Pedro Copa stood to tell of Jack and Roscoe's escape from the mob. Though a small boy at the time, he remembered the fright of the night.

As he told the story we thought of his brother, Cipriano, the boy who went for a cookie, who heard about Jesus, and was converted. Later he attended Bible School, pastored churches for several years, and only recently had been killed when the truck on which he was riding went over the bank on a Yungas road. Seed planted by a missionary with a cookie more than a half century ago, is still producing a harvest among the Aymara.

Since religious leaders instigated the persecution at Karhuisa, we weren't surprised when opposition arose across the mountain behind Copajira. After Carmelo, Mateo, José, and others from that area came to Bible School, they went back to evangelize. Because of their efforts, several groups of new believers began meeting. Eventually, they built church buildings and started schools for their children.

All this growth irritated nonbelievers, especially church leaders. They were extremely upset when they realized that many of the children of that area would not attend their parochial schools. An Italian clergyman from Guaqui incited his parishioners to keep the evangelicals from finishing their church and school buildings at Yauri Korahua.

Dave and Florence Thomas lived at Copajira in 1958. Dave promised to haul rock for the buildings. The morning he went to haul, an angry rock-throwing mob met him. Fortunately, only one believer, standing in the back of the pickup, received a deep cut on the head. Then the mob proceeded to tear down the walls of the church, destroy all the adobes, and carry off all the rocks. So Dave went to La Paz for police protection for believers in Yauri Korahua.

At that time we were planting churches in the Yungas, but fortunately we stopped in La Paz on our way to the farm for special pastor's classes. There Dave met Roscoe and they tramped the streets seeking the necessary official papers guaranteeing protection for believers. Unable to get any such guarantee, we went on to the farm where we heard stories from pastors from across the mountain who had just arrived for classes.

"Pastor, they're plundering our homes," one pled. "They're carrying off our animals and beating us with sticks and whips. Is there no protection?"

A mob of about 400 men guarded roads and roamed across the mountainside in search of believers. Four pastors lost their packs and bicycles when attacked while on their way to classes.

"When they grabbed our *bultos* and bicycles we had a chance to escape," one explained. "They threatened to take us to their church and make us renounce our religion."

Again Dave and Roscoe went back to La Paz in search of protection for these suffering believers.

"The fellows are on their way out to the farm with a commission of soldiers," missionary Catherine Cavit reported on the regular six-o'clock shortwave radio contact that evening. At the farm we listened to her report and rejoiced that help would soon arrive. But they didn't come. Ten o'clock, eleven, midnight...Finally the missionaries slept. Breakfast time came but food didn't sound good.

"Hermano, more pastors from across the mountain have arrived," a student announced. "They say a group of about 500 men from Jesús de Machaca are planning to attack Copajira. More believers have been beaten, and they say they will attack any commission that comes out from La Paz."

At midday with still no sign of the blue farm truck, missionaries were concerned. What had happened if they left last evening? Some thought they might have gone on to Yauri Korahua with the soldiers. Others secretly wondered if they had been attacked along the road. And what about all the happenings across the mountain?

Leland Hibbs and Everett Clarkson went to Guaqui to learn that the blue truck had not gone through the traffic control so we all breathed easier thinking they were probably still in La Paz.

Listen to Roscoe's story:

Thursday afternoon Dave and I tramped from office to office, trying to get protection for our believers. Every official, afraid to do anything, shoved us on to the next official. At six o'clock, the hour to communicate with the farm, we thought we had a promise of a commission. "No, *Señor* Knight," one official said, shaking his head, "I'm afraid there will be bloodshed if we send soldiers, so I withdraw my offer."

Dave and Roscoe didn't give up, but doggedly tramped from office to office until 7:30 that evening, with no success.

Next morning bright and early Roscoe awoke with an idea.

"Maybe the Minister of Agriculture will help," he explained to Dave. "He was a good friend to help when we had problems in the Yungas recently."

They drove down to Calacoto, arriving before the Minister was out of bed.

After introductions, the maid who answered the door disappeared for a moment, then promptly returned.

"Do come in. The *Señor* wants to see you if you are the *Señor* Knight from Coripata in the Yungas."

With the customary greeting and polite chitchat behind them, the Minister in pajamas said, "You are a gentleman of honor and honesty, *Señor* Knight. What can I do for you?"

Roscoe simply told him what was happening at Yauri Korahua. He also showed a letter believers had given to Dave, written and signed by the Italian clergyman, telling the peasants to beat the evangelicals.

Furious, the Minister commanded his aids to go settle the dispute.

"What has been taken must be returned," he instructed. "That foreigner must be expelled from the country for he is dangerous to our government. I advise you Americans not to go with the commission. I'll send a chauffeur for your truck."

Several days later after pastor's classes had closed, we wrote to family in the States.

"Calm has been restored and we feel the Lord has had His hand in the whole situation. We fully expect the work to grow more in that area because of the persecution."

As for the Knights, we went back to plant churches in the Yungas where persecution was not uncommon.

The following month opposition to the Gospel halted another tent meeting. This time it happened not too far from Copajira.

Lucas Condi lived on *hacienda* Guarayo. David Thomas described Lucas as "a small man with smiling black eyes, a bristly mustache, and the grin of a mischievous boy." He loved the Lord and longed to see his neighbors love Him too. After he badgered Dave for a tent meeting in his community, right when Dave was involved with Bible School and had no time for extra meetings, Dave finally gave in, delivered the tent and equipment along with a couple of Bible School evangelists to Lucas' community.

Thirty-four years later we attended a pastor's seminar for those from the Cordillera Quarterly Meeting. At lunchtime we sat on a bench out in the sun to eat soup with the brethren. I struck up a conversation with Roberto, on my left. He said he graduated from Copajira Bible School.

"What do you know about the old green tent?" I asked.

"I was there when it was destroyed," he answered.

"Tell me about it." I scribbled notes as he talked between bites of toasted pasta soup.

"We set up the tent in Condi's patio. He tethered his burros and oxen on the other side of his house then swept the place clean. He was proud to think the missionary would let him have a meeting in his community."

"Did he have a family?" I interrupted.

"Yes, he had a faithful wife and one little boy. I don't know where they were converted nor how long they had been believers." Roberto picked out a piece of bone with his fingers, chewed on it, then continued his story.

"He was anxious to win his neighbors to the Lord but they wouldn't listen to him. While we were pitching the tent he told us how the people of that community were antagonistic toward the Gospel.

"'I've been stoned,' he said. 'They tear up tracts I give them and don't want to listen to my testimony. That's the reason I wanted the tent. Maybe they will listen when someone else in the tent tells of Jesus.'

"We had meetings two nights but Timoteo and I felt the tension in the crowd—a bad spirit," Roberto went on to explain. "Rumors circulated every night. People were uneasy. Finally, the last night a bad group came to listen. The meeting had barely started when we heard something like an Indian war whoop. Then a murmur passed over the entire group. Someone shot a gun or maybe it was dynamite. I don't know—there was lot of confusion. Rocks sailed through the air. Others gathered straw and lit a fire under the side of the tent. Still others came prepared, they lit rags. Condi tried to stop them but they chased him so we ran with him and barricaded ourselves inside his house."

"How long were you in there?" I asked.

"I don't remember. It seemed like a long time. We could hear them trying to burn the tent but it wouldn't burn. That made them angry so they cut it to pieces, cut away the ropes, and pulled up the stakes. They bent the projector and dumped the Bible slides out on the ground. They tried to take the generator but it was too heavy so they pounded it with rocks. Finally, it died and all was dark.

"They beat on Condi's door with stakes, trying to get in. We cried out to the Lord. Then all of a sudden they ran. All was quiet. We didn't go out for a long time until we were sure they had gone."

Dave and Carol Hibbs had gone to pick up the tent that evening, hoping to arrive in time for a part of the meeting. Outside Tiahuanacu someone flagged them down. Dave described the encounter:

He was obviously excited, but not drunk as I had first supposed when he appeared waving wildly in the light of the headlights.

"They have attacked tonight, pastor!" he shouted breathlessly. "They're all drunk." He gulped a mouthful of air and went on. "They've lowered the tent...they are tearing it up with the iron stakes. Listen! You can hear them yelling from here. I don't think you should go any closer." He paused, stepped back and added, "The believers are inside the house in the patio praying."

The whole story seemed fantastic. Guns are seldom really used by the Indians and there had been no hint of violence the night before. We had secured legal permission for the meeting and it was due only to the persistent invitation of Lucas that we had consented to bring the tent during this busy time. Reports can be so exaggerated and as for hearing the mob this far away, I was highly skeptical.

But we stopped again when still at least a mile away, cut the motor, switched off the lights, and got out to listen. There was no doubt now. Drifting across the chill night air we could catch the unmistakable war cries, the shots and shouts of drunken Indians.

Around midnight Lucas arrived (at Copajira), making the usual three-hour walk in half that time. His information was meager but apparently the crowd had seen our headlights, which diverted them for a moment, and seizing the opportunity, the two tent workers and Lucas escaped.

As we ate the second course of our meal, rice covered with tripe and hot tomato sauce, Roberto finished his story:

"Lucas cried when he told Pastor David that the tent was gone. He felt it was his fault they had destroyed it.

"Pastor David told him it wasn't his fault. He said it had served well in the work, had been in 30 evangelistic campaigns, in six camp meetings, been used for many conferences and as a meeting place for unfinished church buildings."

The Old Green Tent had served its purpose and God would supply another.

The old green tent.

The old tent torn to pieces.

11

ESCAPE

The flame of nationalism spread like wildfire across the high plains of the Andes, jumping from *hacienda* to *hacienda*. For centuries there had been boundary disputes between farms. Even though we did everything possible to keep peace with neighboring farms, inevitably trouble raised its ugly head occasionally. Guns, clubs, stones, and alcohol exacerbated the problems during these times. On one such troublesome day a crowd gathered on Copajira to plan strategy for settling the feud.

With only the Cammack family and less than a dozen Bible School students in the compound that Sunday afternoon, all seemed quiet. Suddenly Paul noticed several animals pasturing on Copajira land about a mile below the house.

"Marybel, come go with me. Let's see who owns those animals."

Paul and daughter, in the Jeep station wagon, drove down to investigate the situation. When confronted with the owner of the farm, the *peons* turned their fury from the boundary situation to Paul.

Phyllis, watching from the house, described what happened:

The Jeep, now more than a mile from the compound, was surrounded. A reservoir of hatred toward all farm owners, white people and foreigners exploded. The Jeep was shattered with rocks and clubs, every window demolished.

...Paul hurriedly crawled into the front seat again and called to Marybel, who was under the dashboard, to get out (he meant to say "stay in"), so she opened the door and began to run across the field. Paul tried to start the motor but it was difficult with the rocks flying. It finally started and he took off.

The Indians ran after the car, one with a gun, shooting. With Paul escaping, the crowd sort of forgot Marybel. Paul drove with his head down, so was weaving badly and I thought, "Oh...he is hurt!" Marybel ran to hide behind a bank of the riverbed nearby and Daniel, who had been watching, rushed down with the truck to assist. They found her uninjured—more shaken from seeing her father stoned than from personal injury...

Once in the compound they locked the gates and prepared for any siege that

might occur. That night the crack of rifle
shots split the stillness. Paul, Daniel, and
Leslie McCargue (short-term missionary),
with the Bible School students, walked
throughout the compound all night.

Phyllis and the children, praying, spent the night
in the inner hallway, safe from any stray bullets that
might hit the house. Finally dawn came.

"Daniel and I are going to Guaqui to get help,"
Paul encouraged Phyllis at daybreak Monday morning. "We won't be gone long. Get ready, and I'll take
you and the children to La Paz when we get back."

A short time later they came back, only to encounter the mob waiting in the road. Unable to get
to the house, Daniel jumped out to sneak into the
compound by the back way, while Paul went on to
La Paz to get help.

When Phyllis saw Paul could not get back to the
house she followed the advice of the maid.

"Let's go across to Lacoyo to my house," Jesusa
begged. "You'll be safe there."

Julián and family received them warmly but soon
Daniel arrived, out of breath, saying Indians chased
him and they should move on because of threats
against their lives.

Leaving Lacoyo that evening, they hurried on
across the fields, over hills to another farm.

Again Phyllis tells the story:

We had to cross a high ridge...up we
went, fast. "Mama, can you hurry a little?
They are coming. Come on, can I help
you?"

So on we would go a few more steps, and again we rested. Up, up. Finally, when I felt my lungs may have already burst, we were on top of the mountain. On top of the world! What a view! But no one appreciated it...We must go on.

A Bible School boy had caught up with us so we were a party of six. Where to go? To Guarayo where the tent had been torn up?

We decided to go there to stay with a believer. It was some 12 to 15 miles from the farm I guess...

Lucas Condi graciously bedded them down on the floor of the church between colorful homespun wool blankets. The next day David Thomas found them and returned them to Copajira where Paul was waiting with police officials. They hurriedly packed a few belongings and Phyllis and the children moved to La Paz.

This was the beginning of the end for Copajira, although we didn't know it at the time. Only Paul suspected there might be dark days ahead. When the *peons* complained about his selling sheep to merchants from La Paz Paul envisioned more serious problems. With *chuño* and *tunta* bins full he thought, *What would I do if the peons tried to prohibit my selling our crops?* So, occasionally he took a truckload to sell in La Paz. When someone mentioned that the Caterpillar tractor belonged to the *peons*, Paul laid awake at night wondering how he could get it off the farm.

About that time an army official from Guaqui arrived one morning, "*Señor* Cammack, we need someone to level our soccer field at the army base. Could you do that for us?"

Paul wasn't in the habit of leveling soccer fields but he jumped at the chance to level this one. It would help him get the tractor away. After finishing the job, he loaded the tractor onto the truck and took it to La Paz. Little did he realize the problems he solved for future missionaries on the farm.

Conditions on Copajira continued to deteriorate.

"Our sons don't have land. You didn't give us enough," the *peons* accused us, so we gave them more.

Little by little demands whittled Copajira down to the compound and just 300 acres. Sometimes this whittling process caused extra tension. During one such time Paul asked Roscoe to come out from the Yungas to help measure land for the *peons*. They demanded much larger plots of land, but the missionaries refused to meet their demands. At one point in the vociferous disagreement, someone on the mountain shot a few rounds with his tommy gun, adding to the tenseness of the situation.

On the surface things seemed to sail along smoothly after the *peons* received more land. Underneath they had a growing desire to have the entire farm and be rid of the foreigners—a desire spurred on by the nationalistic spirit in the country. This spirit, kept alive by four congresses led by communists, promised a utopia to the country people.

"Liquidate all foreign landowners!"

"Confiscate the farms!"

"Seize control of the army and customs houses!"

"BOLIVIA FOR THE BOLIVIANS!"

While attending these congresses a communist agitator, Señor Limachi, stirred the imaginations of Copajira nationals:

"Why do these foreigners stay on here? Look how they have exploited the land and the people. The land belongs to the people!

"They gained everything they have on Copajira from the land and since the land belongs to the people, the machinery, produce, animals, and houses also belong to the people. Nothing leaves Copajira and above all, no machinery goes—it belongs to the people.

"They can't have a Bible School anymore. That's against us and the beliefs of our fathers."

"With such propaganda and seeming blessings from the government," Roscoe wrote to the Mission Board, "you can perhaps understand why Copajira nationals believe they have been wronged and that everything belongs to them."

Missionaries were on the move during 1960 and '61. In spite of the unrest, Mark and Wilma Roberts, on furlough, went back to Bolivia; Gene and Betty Comfort and Oscar and Ruth Brown, new appointees, joined the staff; David and Florence Thomas moved to Amacari to carry on evangelism on the peninsula; Paul and Phyllis Cammack moved to Juli, Peru, to begin a new work; and we Knights went back to Bolivia to plant more churches in the Yungas.

When Cammacks left, Mark and Wilma moved to the farm, where he took charge of the farming operation. Within a short time the *peons* made harsh demands, refused to work, demanded their pay without fulfilling their contract and threatened Mark.

"Plow land for us or you'll get what Paul got."

Fortunately for Mark when they asked for more land, he could say, "I'll have to talk to Roscoe. He's the legal representative."

"CPN8FC, CPN8FC, CPN8FC," the shortwave in the Yungas crackled one evening at the usual six o'clock contact.

"There's more trouble at the farm," Mark shouted. "Can you come out for a meeting tomorrow?"

Since Roscoe had a meeting scheduled for the next evening, he invited Mark and Everett Clarkson to come to the Yungas. They arrived at ll:30 p.m., talked until 1:00 a.m. then left before dawn.

The missionary men held many unscheduled meetings to discuss problems such as one with Limachi. Limachi, the chief agitator of the peons, controlled the syndicates that had been organized by the communists on all the *haciendas*.

"Señor, I came out to buy potatoes. Now take me back to Guaqui," he demanded of Mark.

Trying to keep peace, Mark grudgingly consented to do so. On the way to town Limachi demanded that he stop where two women waited by their bundles of produce. Limachi insisted their bundles belonged to him. When Mark got out to help load their *bultos*, Limachi tried to start the Jeep, planning to steal it. It took some fast work and a tussle on Mark's part to regain control.

The *peons* trusted Limachi and thought he wanted to help them but when he later demanded fifty acres of land and the Farmall tractor, they forced him off the farm at gunpoint.

"If you come back, you're dead," Celestino shouted.

About this time we discovered a spy in our midst—wearing the cloak of a believer while exciting the *peons* to take over the farm. Cayetano, a Bible School graduate, had been a pastor and worked for the farm for several years. He had been Paul's right-hand man with the machinery but now set his heart on running it for the *peons* after we were gone.

The missionaries trusted Cayetano and were shocked to hear he was living in sin with Robertses' servant girl. He later stole from them and someone saw him dead drunk at a fiesta. They promptly fired him but this merely spurred him to even greater revenge on the missionaries. We do not know how long Cayetano played the role of a traitor before being caught but evidently for several months.

Not everyone opposed the missionaries. On one occasion Limachi ordered all syndicate leaders of the area to meet at the end of our farm road. More than 1,500 people came for the meeting. He proposed that everyone join with the Copajira syndicate to attack our compound.

"Let's band together to get these foreigners off our land," Eluterio shouted, trying to kindle support for Limachi's plan.

"Why kick them off the land? They supply grain when we don't have food," someone defended.

"Where will we get medicine for our sick when they are gone?"

"Yes, who will come to our houses when we can't walk to a doctor?"

"Mark my word, we'll be sorry when they're gone."

"Eluterio, if you want to help," Limachi suggested, "here's a rifle. We appoint you watchman here at the end of the road. We don't want any animals or machinery to leave this farm."

Accepting the rifle Eluterio declared, "When we take the farm we can go back to our old ways, the ways of our grandfathers."

"Back to the ways of the witch doctor," Rufino added.

"And back to our old religion."

"I will never go back," Ignacio said, shaking his head vigorously.

"Nor I," Pedro added. "I'll never go back to the old ways."

"Just wait and see," Ignacio warned them. "God will punish you for what you are doing to the missionaries."

After three hours of argument they trailed off over the hills to their homes.

Ignacio's warning about God's punishment proved prophetic.

During the growing season the following year a devastating hailstorm destroyed everyone's crops except his and Pedro's.

"I harvested two tons of potatoes from my field," Ignacio related, "I sold to others when they needed food."

Gene and Betty Comfort moved to the farm in time for harvest in 1961. Although Oscar and Ruth Brown lived in La Paz, they too went to the farm to help in the harvest. With Paul in Peru, the task fell to Mark, Gene, and Oscar.

"Don Marcos," someone called softly one night shortly after the light plant had turned off. Grabbing his flashlight, Mark padded to the door to find Cipriano, a Bible School boy, standing in the shadows.

"Turn off the light," Cipriano whispered, "I don't want anyone to know I'm here. A young believer from Sullcata came with disturbing news this evening."

"Oh, what's up?" Mark asked.

"At a joint syndicate meeting in Guaqui today Limachi outlined a plan for taking our farm," Cipriano explained. "An armed group from Lacoyo, Sullcata, and Copajira plan to wait until the missionaries have finished the harvest then raid the compound during full moon. They plan to confiscate our machinery and produce and put the missionaries out on the road with just their suitcases."

We had heard rumors before but coming from Cipriano, a reliable believer, this sounded more authentic. After council meeting the fellows met Paul at Desaguadero on the Peruvian border where they agreed our farming days were over. We would try to keep the compound and a little ground around it for future Bible School gardens but would give all the rest to the *peons*. We also decided all the machinery should be taken off at the close of harvest—a decision that almost cost the menfolk their lives.

12

GOODBYE COPAJIRA

"Cheer up! Not one of us will lose our lives even though the ship will go down."

Wilma Roberts sat quietly pondering the words in Acts 27 during her morning devotions. As she read the story of the apostle Paul's shipwreck, God's word to Paul comforted her when she compared his experience with that of Copajira that morning.

Mark's life had been threatened. Other missionary women had abandoned the farm for safety in La Paz, and truckloads of personal goods found their way to La Paz during the night.

A few days later Mark and Wilma decided time had come for Wilma and the three kids to go to La Paz. After packing a few possessions into their Jeep station wagon, Mark walked down the driveway to unlock the large metal gate. He heard a honk and looked around to see the Jeep coming at him with no appearance of stopping. He barely got out of the way before it crashed into the gate.

"Oh, no! No brakes! There's no time to fix brakes now..." He gave his wife a quick lesson on driving without brakes and commended her to the Lord as she drove off toward the steep, curvy Tambillo hill and on to La Paz where she inched her way down the winding, traffic-laden streets filled with people, to the mission house.

Back at the farm only Mark, Oscar, and Gene stood by to bring in the harvest. Rumors kept everyone tense. Neighboring communities wanted the compound for a boarding school for primary and high school students. The *peons* had signed papers saying they wouldn't ask for more land but now they wanted our homes.

Missionaries felt like prisoners on their own farm. The *peons* declared that all animals and machinery belonged to them as rightful owners of the farm so watched every move for fear "their" property would be taken from the farm. They also threatened missionaries were that to happen. When Mark sold 150 merino sheep, *peons* accused the new owner of thievery as he drove his new property down the road.

Hearing rumors of an attack by *campesinos* of both Copajira and the neighboring communities, Mark, Gene, and Oscar hastened to finish harvest. From sunup until dark they dug potatoes, harvested barley, and filled bins in the warehouse. As Oscar drove the combine around and around the field he pondered the question Damaso had asked.

"*Señor*, are you going to finish the harvest?"

"This was a difficult question to answer in truth," Oscar wrote later, "because our plan was to finish all except one field of poorer grain, then take the machinery off the farm under cover of darkness. How could I answer?

"I could only say, `I'm afraid we can't get it all. The grain is down badly.'"

While the peons thought of a material harvest, Oscar thought of a spiritual one—would there be a harvest of souls on Copajira? For 13 years missionaries had faithfully sown the seed of the Gospel. During those 13 years Friends churches of the Northwest had prayed for a harvest of souls. Fertile soil had produced several small groups of believers in the surrounding area; would Copajira remain unproductive? True, Pedro, Ignacio, Crisóstomo, and Luís had believed at one time but now, under pressure, had they turned away from the Lord? Only time would tell.

Early morning shadows fled down the Yungas canyon as we Knights wound our way up the narrow ribbon of road. Breaking through the mist spilling over the ridge just below Unduavi, we found bright sunlight, deep blue sky, jagged cliffs, and snow-covered mountain peaks— a stark contrast to our jungle green canyon. Here we pulled our sweaters closer, remembering that the last of May on the *altiplano* could bring frost, a skim of ice on water, and crisp cold mornings.

"How long will we have to be here in La Paz?" one of the children asked in a tone of voice that expressed their dislike for the incarceration in the city.

"We don't know," Roscoe answered. "Probably several days since we may have to settle farm problems."

Problems proved to be serious. In spite of threats, the mission council approved taking the big machinery off the farm, so Everett and Roscoe went to the farm to help finish the harvest.

"We'll contact you by radio at six o'clock as usual," they called as they drove out the gate.

Children played in the backyard. We womenfolk busied ourselves with settling kid squabbles, knitting, visiting, cooking, eating—anything to keep our minds off the danger at the farm.

"CPN8FB..CPN8FB.., come in CPN8FB."

Static drowned out all radio contact so our imaginations ran wild. Friday, the target date for leaving the farm, came and went, with no word. Had someone discovered our plan? Had the missionary men been attacked? Why the delay?

Finally, through the pop and crack of static, we thought we heard the word "safe." With that bit of uncertain news, we slept.

At the farm on Friday *peons* pushed for more land so the fellows gave them all except the compound and 25 acres for the Bible School. Contented, but using the old Latin technique of "it never hurts to ask," the *peons* milled around the compound all day trying to wheedle more things from these generous missionaries—seed potatoes, sheep, machinery, school equipment, whatever. Little did they realize that behind that generosity lay the urge to quickly finish sorting potatoes, cut the grain, then load the truck and pickup for a quick getaway the next morning.

Trusty Bible School students, Cipriano and Segundino, worked alongside the missionaries, not realizing the urgency of the situation. Their only thought was to finish the harvest.

"They must not know our plans," someone remarked, "for the *peons* will be mad enough to kill when we are gone. We don't want the boys to get blamed for helping us escape."

"A fire is burning up on the cliff," Segundino said, as he returned from outside the compound to sort more potatoes.

"Oh?"

Who was it—a spy? Had someone discovered their plan? Only glances communicated any fear, for fires had been a signal for attack in times past.

"I'll go see what's up," Cipriano offered, glad to leave the potato bins.

"Just someone stealing potatoes," he reported after his short scouting foray.

With a soft chuckle that signaled relief, everyone hurried to finish their jobs.

After the guards went to bed, missionary men quietly loaded the pickup with small mechanical tools, gas and electric motors, welding equipment, and other objects of value. All was ready for an early start the next morning. They fell into bed about 12:30 but slept little.

At four a.m., June 3, 1961, five missionary men tumbled out of bed, dressed warmly to brave a chilly morning, ate a hasty breakfast, then headed for the machine lot. All felt tense as they made a final check making sure everyone remembered the escape plan.

The men planned that motors would start simultaneously after the first pop of the John Deere tractor. The starter on the diesel ground away but Gene couldn't get a spark out of it. Everyone held their breath wondering why the delay. What had gone wrong?

Ah, no fuel in the starting motor! After a quick fill, the motors roared into action, making more noise than they had ever remembered before. The sound wafted across the crisp morning air, echoing back from the cliff below.

Roscoe swung the gates open to wave them out. Oscar led the way on the combine. Gene followed on the John Deere pulling the large hydraulic-lift disk. Mark pulled out next in the International truck with the platform scales balanced on the last full load of barley. Everett finished the parade in the blue pickup. Roscoe hurriedly clicked the padlock on the gate and hopped in with Everett.

"We were off in a parade of suspense!" Oscar described it later. "Down the hillside back of the sheep feedlot, across the river and up the hill opposite the compound. I looked back to see a grotesque train of machinery moving slowly in the early morning moonlight."

"At last we were on our way," Roscoe recounted the experience. "The sight of lightless vehicles creeping through the dark made chills run up and down my spine. As we pulled out into the main road we looked back on Copajira, quiet, still sleeping in the early dawn, unconscious of the fact that the machinery was on its way to La Paz."

Several miles from the farm Everett and Roscoe decided to go back to see the reaction of their leaving. Two boys met them, saying angry, armed men occupied the compound, so the fellows decided against going any closer.

Four and a half hours later, while eating lunch in La Paz, a tired, dirty, hungry but happy group of five missionaries regaled their wives with the suspense and excitement of the morning.

After a short rest curiosity got the best of the men so they drove back the fifty miles to find out the results of their escape. They feared looters would carry away everything. Hoping someone along the road could give them a report, they waited, but nobody came. So they drove closer. Still no one. Around the last little knoll, within sight of the compound, they shared binoculars to watch people milling around inside.

"Look, mirrors flashing up on the cliff!"

"Hey, there's a flash from *Tata* Luís' house too!"

As they watched, someone waved a large red blanket from Luís' patio.

"It's a warning from *Tata* Luís. We'd better not go any farther."

A panting Cipriano arrived a few minutes later. "Everything is calm in the compound. The *peons* sent me to say it is okay, you can come up. They won't hurt you."

Noticing the sun about to drop over the Peruvian hills, and knowing night would follow shortly, the men felt uneasy about entering the compound.

"We'd better head back to La Paz."

Early Sunday morning, taking Gene's Jeep station wagon, they drove back to the farm. They felt good, for hadn't Cipriano said everything was calm? On the way they sang old hymns and felt encouraged and fearless as they approached the compound.

Suddenly the general secretary of the farm stepped through the little side gate brandishing a rifle.

"Celestino, put that gun down!" Roscoe ordered.

"Get in here or I'll shoot your tires," he barked as he lowered the gun to the Jeep's tires.

"Celestino, put that gun down!" Roscoe ordered the second time.

Segundino, a Bible School boy, opened the big wrought iron gate. As the missionary men drove through, a drunken mob leapt from behind the Russian olive trees wildly waving rifles.

Roughly forcing the missionaries out of the Jeep, they pushed, pulled, pinched, and knocked them about. Then frisking them, they left their billfolds but took their keys.

Mark, responsible for the farm, resisted.

"Let's get rid of that guy," someone said.

Understanding their Aymara, Roscoe said, "Mark, give them the keys."

With rifles at the ready they marched the men through the compound to the empty machine lot.

"Where's the machinery? Why didn't you ask us if you could take it? What do you mean sneaking off at night? Don't you have confidence in us? Don't you trust us?"

Everyone talked at once as they waved rifles, whips, and clubs. Alcohol flowed freely in the background, helping to fuel the anger of about 70 men to a frightening level.

"Kill them!" some shouted. "Kill the *gringos*! Don't let them get away!"

Noting the missionaries showed little fear, some started fighting between themselves with whips and clubs and others shot into the air.

Mark argued with them but it only made the *peons* more angry.

"Let's kill him," someone said in Aymara.

"Be quiet, Mark," Roscoe spoke sharply. Quietly he added, "I'm not sure we'll get out of this alive." As spokesman for the group, he found his mouth dry, almost too dry to speak the difficult guttural Aymara language.

"What do you have to say?" Celestino demanded.

"Since you have taken most of the land, we have no use for the big machinery so we took it to La Paz," Roscoe explained.

This simple truth quieted their frenzy of questions and threats. The *peons* drew apart to discuss the situation, leaving the missionary men a chance to make a fast decision. Being in a poor position to bargain, they found it difficult to make a decision while looking down the barrel of a rifle.

"Well, how do you want to settle this?" Celestino demanded.

After much argument the *peons* presented simple conditions: "Give us the land, houses, and the machinery that is here (which, fortunately, was old equipment of little value), and we will not let anyone steal from your houses and will let you take out your own personal goods and take half the potatoes, barley, and sheep. We want the titles to the land, and no missionaries can live here again."

With the mob becoming more violent, their tempers shorter, and their guns threatening, the missionaries agreed to the *peons'* demands.

The *peons* cheered when they heard the agreement. Crisóstomo jumped on the old Farmall tractor and spun it around in circles, making everyone run for their lives.

The missionaries, however, set their terms for taking things from the farm.

"We'll keep this agreement if only ten men are present in the compound, if there are no guns, and if no one is drinking."

The *peons* agreed. Later we learned they had stashed 30 rifles in the sheep corral and many more men waited outside the walls, drinking.

"We know *Señor Raúl* is honest and will keep his word, so you may go now," Celestino nodded.

What a relief! After standing tense and fearful as prisoners for two hours, listening to threats, fights, and rifle fire, praying, wondering if they would be held hostage, and finally, bargaining for their lives, they could leave. They filed through the compound to the Jeep to discover three cameras, one pair of binoculars, and one razor gone. A small loss in the face of reality.

Early Monday morning the men went to the Alto to move the machinery to a safer place. Since they had confessed the day before to having taken it to La Paz, they feared the *peons* would come searching. They did.

After a search of our tabernacle property on the Alto, the *peons* came to the house. "You lied to us. The machinery isn't there. We demand the machinery and the titles to the farm."

The missionaries had already decided to be firm. "You will not get the titles to the farm if you do not keep your part of the agreement we made yesterday," Roscoe declared. Later the *peons* brought their lawyer, who wrote out the agreement and witnessed the signing by both the *peons* and the missionaries.

Roscoe could hardly bear the thought of signing away Copajira. It had been his dream from the beginning—a Bible School on the farm where young Aymaras could study to become better pastors, workers, teachers, and leaders in the church.

Life had to go on so early Wednesday morning seven trucks, the missionary men, and 15 believers went to the farm to recover personal property. Wilma went to help pack her things. Ruth and I asked to go also.

"No!" our husbands replied firmly.

When the group arrived at the farm, missionaries, believers, and truck drivers worked feverishly to remove as much as possible. *Peons*, guarding all the buildings—four houses, warehouse, shop, and school—contested everything they attempted to take.

"No, that belongs to the farm!"

"Don't touch that, it's ours."

To make matters worse, the *peons* would not deal with believers or missionaries, only Roscoe.

When some *peons* wouldn't let Wilma take her own curtains, she shoved them out the door and continued packing. Being a woman, she could get away with it.

The *peons*, begging and stealing, dropped everything they stole or were given over the compound wall into the arms of wives or children waiting on the other side.

Nícolas, believer and carpenter, went into the shop to get blades for the planer.

"Get out," *peons* yelled, as they whacked him on the shoulder with a board then chased him across the compound.

Roscoe feared someone would be killed. "Don't touch a thing until I have bargained with the *peons*."

"You can't take that," someone warned Everett, when he started taking the old telephone off the wall.

"Why not? You can't use this. It only speaks English."

With no resistance the antique telephone found a place on the truck.

Late that evening back in La Paz, Ruth and I went to the tabernacle at the Alto to watch truck after truck arrive, loaded with furniture, machinery, grain, potatoes, and a believer perched high on top as guard of each truck.

I don't know how others felt, but I cried. Copajira, the Bible School, our homes, friends, hopes for the future—all gone. At that moment I could not see the blessing of our loss.

After a rough day of having to argue for everything, some of the missionary men were dubious about going back another day even though they hadn't gotten their share of the produce. With a good night's rest, however, they all felt they should try again.

Because of threats and rough treatment the day before, only two believers braved the trip again with the missionaries and six trucks. Seven men sacked and loaded grain and potatoes all day. They worked hard, not even taking time for lunch.

"That's half—no more," Victoriano commanded as they sacked potatoes from the bins.

"No, it isn't. That's barely a fourth," Roscoe argued as he measured on the side of the bin.

So the men sacked a few more.

"That's enough!"

"But it's only a third of the bin."

All morning they argued for every inch they got from the produce bins. By early afternoon the *peons* became sullen, began drinking and tempers flared. Roscoe pushed them to the limit but knew when to stop, fearing a fight.

They divided the sheep, giving the mission ten less than half, then exchanged scrawny ones for the best of our flock of merinos.

The climax came when the missionaries started to clean out the clinic. *Peons* got tired of watching "their" possessions leave the farm. Someone said the wrong thing, which threatened to cause a fight.

"We <u>will</u> take these tooth extractors and the microscope," Roscoe said determinedly, as he picked them up and left the room. The others followed. Nerves stretched to the breaking point.

"Let's go. We've loaded six trucks today. That's enough."

The missionary men got into the Jeep, pulled out of the compound, and started to follow the trucks down the road.

"Stop!" Mark cried. "I forgot my dogs."

"Forget it. Let them go."

"I can't. They won't have anything to eat."

Mark jumped out and ran back to find the dogs. The others sat tense, wanting to get out fast for fear someone would start shooting, but now they waited for Mark and his dogs.

With no room for two big dogs, Mark pushed them into the Jeep to sit on missionary laps. Since they had never ridden in a vehicle before and fought to get out, Mark finally opened the door and let them go home.

Meanwhile, in La Paz, the womenfolk worried.

"They said they'd not be late today; they'd be here by four o'clock," someone reminded us.

"I wish we had radio contact."

I walked up and down the driveway. My imagination ran wild. Had they been ambushed? Were they held hostage with no way of letting us know? Had fighting broken out? I imagined the injured and dying. Why don't they come? I could only pray.

"Lord, it's your farm. We're your servants. You've promised not to leave us nor forsake us so cover them with Your hand of protection. Bring them home safely."

He answered and we praised Him!

Later Roscoe wrote an analytical report of the Copajira situation for the Mission Board:

...We went to no officials at first because we knew if we did, we would lose everything by theft. Also, if we had asked for armed officials, had we been able to obtain them, there would have been bloodshed...The government is afraid to move in the country areas, thus there is no law.

After we took 13 truckloads off Copajira I went to see the Minister of Indian Affairs. He was ill (I would be too if I had his job), but I talked to his assistant. After giving them my report they said there were no guarantees for those who live in country areas. I then went to the American Embassy. They were thankful we had escaped with our lives and thought we were extremely fortunate to have retrieved so much of our personal goods and machinery from the farm.

We were allowed to return home unharmed on Sunday because they believed our word that we would fulfill our promise to them. Since I have worked with them from the beginning, they still looked to me as the owner and said that my word was good. Thus I felt that a Quaker's word must be as good as his bond and that even though we had made the promises under duress, we had to fulfill them.

Previously, I said that I would never sign the titles over to them, but sometimes you do things under force that you would not do otherwise.

I've spent many hours thinking about this and am still convinced that we did the best thing. To us it seems nothing but highway robbery. To them, they gave us a good deal. They've been made to believe that the land is theirs and that we have made our fortune from it. They actually believed that the land, machinery and crops were rightfully theirs. They condemned those who stole our cameras that Sunday.

"That's bad. They're thieves."

Later we learned that while they were talking to us, Señor Limachi, the communist leader, tried to cross wires on Gene's Jeep to steal it. Earlier he had ordered the farm Indians to confiscate the Jeep but they refused.

176

I am sure that some still have consciences and know down deep in their hearts they are wrong but they will not admit it now. Limachi said he could muster thousands of men to bring order to Copajira. That isn't an idle threat for we have various points against us—we are foreigners, we are Americans, we are evangelicals, we are wealthy landowners. No matter how we look at it, it is true...by their standards we are rich, we have exploited them by using their land and giving them nothing in return.

We considered fighting it legally but are convinced that in the long run it would do more harm than good for the mission work. We have lost nothing but material goods. "The Lord giveth and the Lord taketh away." And by the way, He will give again when we need it.

We are still free to work that whole area. They so completely believed our word that had we broken it, they would not trust us again. I'm convinced that we will someday win more souls for the Lord right on Copajira. I've been concerned as to the effect this could have on the national church.

We are still convinced that Copajira was purchased under God's direction, that it has served its purpose as a home for the Bible School, and has been the means of training many men for God's work, as well as being a base for the establishment of churches in that area. Due to the rapidly changing conditions in Bolivia, however, those days are past, as well as many of our systems and ways of doing missionary work. Our missionary approach needs to be highly flexible so as to change with the conditions within the country. Only in this way can we continue working here. May God give us wisdom!

Goodbye Copajira

13

GROWING PAINS

The loss of Copajira and the Bible School seemed a tragedy at the time but it actually provided another step in the development of the Bolivian national church. Although we cried at the time, God had a plan for the situation.

Early missionaries worked tirelessly to expedite the goals of evangelizing the Aymara people, establishing a strong national church, and training national workers. Carrol Tamplin rode a motorcycle across the *altiplano* and sailed a boat around the islands of Lake Titicaca spreading the Gospel.

Helen Cammack rode a feisty mule, Princess, and later a more docile one, Yanapiri (Helper), throughout the Puerto Perez/Batallas area, passing out gospel tracts at markets, visiting, encouraging, teaching Bible classes, and conducting children's meetings. Later she started a primary school in La Paz.

Estel Gulley, with her medical skills, doctored the sick.

Howard and Julia Pearson braved the higher altitude of over 13,000 feet to preach the Word among the Aymaras in the Corocoro copper mining area. When they left for furlough Ralph and Marie Chapman assumed leadership roles throughout the field while living in La Paz.

When we arrived in 1945, the mission followed the paternalistic system used by all missions in Bolivia at that time. We hired and fired. We paid the bills. We built churches, paid pastors, directed primary schools, preached, taught, planned conferences, and directed the work in general.

Paternalism smacked of colonialism. It pointed out the inability of the Aymara to direct their own institutions. It accentuated their feelings of inferiority while making the missionary appear superior in their eyes. We soon discovered the fallacy of the paternalistic system and the mission began to make changes.

Even though the Aymara Friends church started on a firm foundation, that of evangelism and education, we soon realized the need for an indigenous church: self-governing, self- propagating, and self-supporting— one that could stand alone if and when the missionary left.

Beginning in 1947, several attempts made at organizing an indigenous church failed. The mission introduced the indigenous church plan but the national leaders vetoed it.

In 1951, Walter Lee, president of Oregon Friends Mission Board, visited Bolivia. Together with missionaries and nationals, he helped initiate a plan whereby the newly formed national Friends Church—INELA—accepted the responsibility of developing a plan for pastoral support. The missionaries would relinquish pastoral positions and cooperate in programs of evangelism and education.

Missionaries helped the nationals develop the organizational structure of the INELA and write a constitution. These improvements strengthened the church, making believers proud of belonging to a national Friends Church.

Had we listened more closely when Clyde Taylor, Executive Director of the Evangelical Foreign Missions Association, spoke to a group of missionaries studying Aymara at Copajira in 1952, we might have anticipated problems.

"The U. S. State Department," Clyde said, "is following with great concern the events taking place in Cuba. Communist forces are training in Cuba, then infiltrating Bolivia to arouse a revolt among peasants. Copajira could be a target."

Later, fellow-missionary Jack Willcuts cautioned the mission council, "Within a few years we will be deciding between the farm and the national church."

The INELA experienced turbulent years in the 1950's. Leaders absconded with church funds; greed caused the downfall of some; and internal conflicts tore the organization apart.

In 1960, while we were in the States on furlough, Roscoe went back to the field with Dean Gregory, General Superintendent of Northwest Yearly Meeting, and Oscar Brown, Mission Board president, to work through problems with the national church.

After one stormy session, church leaders threatened to go to another mission if the Friends mission didn't continue financial support. Knowing that we could not back down on our convictions for the establishment of an indigenous church, Dean stood on the steps of the mission home and with tears streaming down his cheeks, he said, "We've lost it. After all these years, we've lost it."

Some months later, spurred on by the nationalistic spirit of Bolivia, the executive council of the INELA made demands the mission thought were not compatible with an indigenous church. The nationals requested funds for church construction, property purchases, salaries for pastors, workers, and teachers, and a vehicle. This impasse caused the Mission Board to withdraw some missionary families for an early furlough, leaving only a skeleton staff in Bolivia.

The Bible School, the national church, and the farm all felt the effects of both Taylor's and Jack's predictions of nationalistic agitation. A rather vociferous student formed a secret student union within the school. Some members of the INELA supported their demands for a vehicle, the farm income, a normal school, and a theological seminary instead of Bible School. The mission could not meet these demands without upsetting our goals for the church.

Money became the dividing factor between mission and national leaders--money for pastors, teachers, churches, school, vehicles, and much more. Members of the INELA even coveted the farm to use as a means of support for the national church program.

"You gave the farm away to wicked men instead of to the church," one leader, who refused to preach tithing, bitterly accused the missionaries. "Had you given it to us we could have supported our churches with the income."

These critics didn't stop to realize there would have been jealousy and fighting among church leaders. Nor did they realize the *peons* would have killed rather than release one hectare of land.

"Now we see God's blessing in losing the farm," I wrote to the north. "It was the only way we would have let go, and the only way to keep the national church from being split over the situation. God knew best."

Finally, in 1964, Carmelo Aspi, a graduate of Helen Cammack Memorial Bible School, presented a plan challenging the national church executive council to accept responsibility for their own church. This ended 17 years of trial and error, prompting a rapid growth in the church.

Throughout the years 24 missionary couples worked with Aymara leaders to establish an indigenous work in Bolivia. Today Bolivian brethren plant churches, sponsor conferences, and oversee the work in all districts. When the tabernacle collapsed with a heavy snow in June 1975, each district took responsibility for its own Easter Conference. Today missionaries are sometimes guest speakers but more often the executive council loads a tent into their pickup and drives to a distant area where Aymaras preach, teach, counsel, and encourage.

With Copajira Bible School gone, the INELA started their own Bible School. Thus, Patmos was born. The former mission house became headquarters for the INELA, UFINELA (women's organization), UJELAB (youth organization), TEE (Theological Education by Extension), a clinic, and the Patmos Bible Institute.

The success of changing from paternalism to the indigenous system is due largely to much prayer, patience, wisdom, and the united efforts of willing nationals, the missionaries, and the Mission Board.

Today more than 200 Bolivian Friends churches dot the *altiplano*, climb the heights to over 13,000 feet in the Pacajes area on the Peruvian/Chilean border, spill over the Andes into the Yungas and Alto Beni jungle, march on toward the Brazilian border to the frontier town of Santa Cruz and on out into the colonization project of San Julián.

Paul and Phyllis Cammack pioneered in opening a new field on the Peruvian *altiplano*. We followed them, and a succession of missionaries and nationals continue to reap the Peruvian harvest. Today more than 50 churches fan out across the *altiplano* and nestle in the towns along the Pacific coast.

Dare I suggest that under the guidance of the Holy Spirit a small Bible School on Copajira sparked the growth of the national Friends Church of today? Without question, growth must also be credited to the faithful witness of laymen, capable Bible School graduates, the mature leadership of the INELA, and the dogged tenacity of missionaries.

Former mission house—now church headquarters

14

LOOKING BACK

Although many neighboring communities welcomed the missionaries after we lost Copajira, the people of the farm remained antagonistic. We wondered and waited for news. Bits and pieces of news finally leaked out.

Immediate results of losing the farm distressed us. Dissatisfied that they didn't get a pickup in the settlement, the *peons* threatened to confiscate any mission vehicle that came on their land. We knew they couldn't handle a pickup if they had one, for they promptly wrecked the tractor we left them. They went back to plowing with oxen and wooden plow. Maybe it was for the best—it kept them from fighting over who would drive the tractor and who would pay for tractor fuel.

Believers living on Copajira suffered. An 18 year old shepherd arrived at the mission house in La Paz, crying. "I want to go to church, but my dad won't let me. He beat me with a *chicote* and locked me in the corral with the animals but I sneaked out and caught a truck for La Paz."

"What will you do here in town?"

"I have a job as a *cargador*, carrying produce at the *tambo*, the farmer's market," he said proudly.

Every Sunday he faithfully attended service at Max Paredes. Would this young fellow be a part of the harvest to be gathered from Copajira? We remembered ten years earlier when his father had forbidden Francisco, his brother, from attending church and he also had left home. Did Carlos, this domineering father, realize he was driving his boys to the Lord?

Another sad report came to us from a neighboring farm. Cayetano, the Bible School graduate who had driven the tractor and combine for six years on the farm, became bitter and mean when, with the machinery gone, he no longer had a job. He took his spite out on his wife, Jesusa.

"I'll kill you if you ever set foot inside that church again," he threatened, after severely beating her.

"I'm not afraid, Cayetano," she answered defiantly. "I'd be better off if you killed me, then I'd be in Heaven. I'm not afraid of what happens in this world, but I'd be very afraid of what would happen in the next world if I didn't follow my Lord."

At least two *peons* and their families stood faithful to the Lord throughout the persecution—Pedro and Ignacio. We longed to know about Luís, Dionicio, and others who had listened to the Gospel. Had the Seed sprouted? What about the harvest on Copajira?

Since missionaries had not been allowed to set foot on Copajira for more than 20 years, on a trip from Peru to La Paz we Knights dared to visit the compound, hoping the years had wiped away the anger and threats from the *peons*.

On our way up from the main road we stopped to visit *Tata* Luís. He and his wife had been faithful believers at one time but when the farm was taken he sided with the *peons* against the missionaries. We longed to know whether they were coerced or whether they had actually turned their backs on the Lord.

Following a path along the edge of a potato field, we found Luís in a field of golden *quinoa*.

"*Buenas tardes, hermano Luís,*" Roscoe greeted him. With no response of recognition, he continued, "I'm *don* Raúl."

"Who?"

"Don Raúl."

"The *don* Raúl that used to be here at Copajira?"

"Yes."

"*Oh, gracias a Dios.* Thank God you've come," he cried as he stumbled across rows of *quinoa* to embrace us tightly. "You've come, you've come," he sobbed.

After a tearful reunion, Luís, nearly blind, led us across his field. "This is the land I'm giving for a church," he explained, pointing to a piece along the road. "I want them to build it right here. I won't be here but my children and grandchildren will need a place to worship."

After a short visit, prayer, and hugs we left knowing that Luís had made his peace with God. Perhaps he had never turned his back on his Lord, which was evident when he flashed the mirrors and waved the red poncho from his patio as a warning to the missionaries.

Leaving Luís, we stopped to greet a young man along the road. Not knowing what kind of reception we would receive, we kept our car doors locked.

"*Buenas tardes*," Roscoe spoke through my window. "We'd like to visit the farm. I'm *don* Raúl and lived here years ago."

A look of doubt spread across his face, but he went around to the other side to get a closer look.

"You're *don* Raúl? You're the *don* Raúl that lived here?"

"Yes, I'm *don* Raúl."

His face lit up as he exclaimed, "You're my godfather. You named me. I'm Samuel. You gave me my name, Samuelito."

Immediately Roscoe hopped out of the Toyota to give this slightly inebriated young man an *abrazo*. Yes, Roscoe remembered dedicating Samuel when his parents were in the church.

"And your father, Crisóstomo?"

"He died. He drowned when coming home from Guaqui one night."

Crisóstomo had made a start with the Lord during the early years we were on the farm, but he couldn't leave his alcohol. While drunk he drowned in a water ditch.

"Come see my mother. She would like to see you," Samuel urged. Following him along the ridge at the end of a potato field, we arrived at his house to find not only his mother but three drunk friends.

"What have we gotten into?" I asked, more to myself than to anyone else.

Not having a very clear mind, Samuel introduced us to Victoriano, Rufino, and Vicente. All three welcomed us back with warm *abrazos*, then offered us a nip from their bottles. We graciously declined and ducked out from under their embraces as soon as possible.

Samuel followed us back to the car, encouraging us to drive up to the compound. But as we prepared to leave the General Secretary of the farm stopped to greet us. Samuel told him our desires to see the compound but he declined.

"No, you can't go up there. You wouldn't like what you saw."

While driving on to La Paz we analyzed his response. "They're still hard but his remark proves they are ashamed of what they did to us years ago. Probably we will never know what hearts have been changed as a result of the work at Copajira."

We do know, however, of some hearts that were changed. Several months later a cold wind from across the lake swept dust into their eyes as the Secretary of Evangelism and his helpers raised the tattered tent for Quarterly Meeting in Zapana, fifteen miles from Copajira. Believers walked many miles, carrying Bibles, bedding, soup bowls and cups on their backs, then settled down to receive the rich blessings from the Lord. They sang lustily, testified, and listened to messages morning, afternoon, and night, which provided a spiritual feast for all.

Among the many who attended was a nice-looking fellow with a lighter complexion and a receding hairline. "He didn't look quite like he belonged in an *altiplano* meeting," Roscoe described him to me later.

"Do you know who I am?" he asked Roscoe during the supper hour.

"No, I'm afraid I don't."

"I'm Saturnino Choque. I was the public school teacher at Copajira 40 years ago." He paused, waiting for a look of recognition from Roscoe, then plunged on. "I incited the peons to fight for a Catholic school. We wrecked the school building, broke the door down, ruined the windows, and finally took our case to the authorities in La Paz.

"Yes, I faintly remember," Roscoe nodded, remembering a cocky young teacher who had caused lots of trouble.

"You refused to let me teach," Saturnino continued. "Eventually, *don* Pablo and you threw me into the pickup, took me to kilometer seven and told me never to come back." Smiling, Roscoe admitted he remembered that part.

The following afternoon Saturnino stood in meeting and publicly asked pardon of Roscoe. Although he had been converted several years before, now a load lifted, as both he and Roscoe knelt before each other to ask pardon in the typical Aymara way. Today Saturnino pastors the Sullcata Friends Church, which meets on property he gave for that purpose.

A year later we made the trip to the Frontera area for another Quarterly Meeting at San Pedro Tana. As we passed Copajira we marvelled at how the work had grown to 21 churches in that area. Speeding on down the road we passed someone standing alongside, waving his cap frantically.

"That looked like Braulio." Roscoe braked to a stop and backed up.

"*Buenos días, hermano Raúl*," Braulio greeted. "We heard you were going to San Pedro Tana so would like to go with you. We have some business to tend to over there."

"Sure, hop in."

As we jolted along we visited with Braulio, his wife, and his sister-in-law.

The day passed as most Quarterly Meetings with eating, fellowship, singing, reports, preaching, praying, and testimonies. This day, however, was different. Roscoe preached and some were there to transact business with the Lord.

After the altar service Braulio, his wife, and his sister-in-law stayed at the altar to testify. Braulio told of how the Lord had kept him faithful through much persecution at the farm and that perseverance had resulted in a small group of believers and a church building at Copajira.

Braulio's wife told of life on the farm when the missionaries lived there, then kneeling with Roscoe she asked pardon. "I took poles and roofing from the compound when you left years ago. Please forgive me. I can't pay for them, but I want peace in my heart." Then her sister gave the same testimony and asked pardon.

Roscoe gladly forgave them. On our way home we dropped them off at Copajira, realizing the business they needed to tend to that day was that of restitution.

"Can you imagine carrying that weight of guilt for 30 years?" We shook our heads in amazement, marvelling at the Lord's faithfulness.

As we drove back toward La Paz in late evening, the beauty of the *altiplano,* the snowcapped *cordillera* and Mt. Illimani rising above La Paz, all golden with a setting sun, left us misty-eyed with its splendor. With a sense of peace we remembered that God makes the wrath of man to praise Him. Although the farm and Bible School were gone, the results of that seed-sowing time still produce a harvest.

TO GOD BE THE GLORY, GREAT THINGS HE HATH DONE!

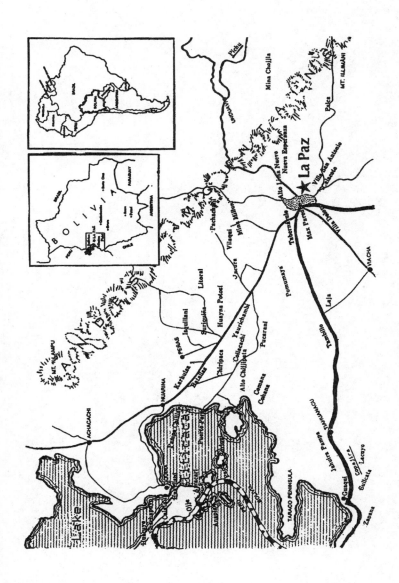

GLOSSARY

Abarcas
(ah-BAHR-cahs)..........Sandals made from old tires, worn
                            by both men and women
Abrazo
(ah-BRAH-so)..............Hug, form of greeting
Ahuayo
(ah-WAH-yo)..............Large square of colorful cloth used
                            by Aymara women for carrying things
                            on their backs
Ají
(ah-HEE)....................Hot chili peppers
Altiplano
(ahl-tee-PLAH-no)......High plains of the Andes
Anafe
(ah-NA-fay)................One burner kerosene cooking stove
Aymara
(ay-MAH-rah)..............Large Indian tribe of the Andes
Balsa
(BAHL-sah)................Reed boat of Lake Titicaca
Brujo
(BRU-ho)....................Witch Doctor
Bulto
(BOOL-to)..................Pack carried on the back
Campesinos
(cahm-pay-SEE-nohs).Country people, farmers
Chicote
(chee-COH-tay)...........Whip
Chuño
(CHEWN-yo)..............Dehydrated freeze-dried potato
Coca
(COH-cah)..................Narcotic plant native to the Yungas
                            from which cocaine is extracted

197

Copajira
(coh-pah-HEE-rah)......3000 acre mission farm situated near
                         Lake Titicaca
Cordillera
(cohr-deel-YER-ah).....The Andean mountain range tower-
                         ing over the Altiplano
Don
(dohn).........................Mister, but used only with first
                         name, showing respect or position
Gorro
(GOH-ro)....................Knit cap with ear flaps, worn by
                         Aymara men
Gringo
(GREEN-go)...............White man
Haba
(AH-bah)....................English lima bean
Hacienda
(ah-see-EN-dah)..........Large farm
Hermana
(air-MAH-nah).............Sister
Hermano
(air-MAH-no)...............Brother
Hombre
(OHM-bray).................Man
INELA
(ee-NAY-lah)...............Acronym for National Evangelical
                         Friends Church
Jichu
(HEE-choo).................Long wiry grass of the high plains
Jilacata
(hee-lah-CAH-tah)......Legal representative and authority
                         of a farm or community
Mama
(MAH-mah)................Married Aymara woman
Mariqueta
(Mah-ree-KAY-tah)......Fist-size loaf of bread, similar to
                         French bread

Max Paredes
(max-pah-RAY-days).....Street on which the central Friends
church is located in La Paz
Mujer
(moo-HAIR)................Woman
Oka
(OH-kah)....................Edible tuber of the potato family
Pachamama
(pah-chah-MAH-mah).Goddess of the earth
Pampa
(PAHM-pah)...............Large flat plain
Patrón
(pah-TROHN).............Farm owner, landlord or boss
Pensión
(pen-see-OHN)...........Small hotel or hostel
Peón
(pay-OHN)..................Serf, unskilled laborer
Poncho
(POHN-cho)...............Woolen cloak like a blanket with slit
in center for the head
Quena
(KAY-nah)...................Reed flute
Quinoa
(KEEN-wah)...............Small round grain of the high plains,
highly nutritious
Raúl
(rah-OOL)...................Roscoe's spanish name
Sampoña
(sahm-POHN-yah)......Flute with many pipes of varying
sizes; panpipe
Sultana
(sool-TAH-nah)...........Husk of the coffee bean
Tata
(TAH-tah)...................Aymara for father or man
Tola
(TOH-lah)...................Bush similar to sage brush

Totora
(toh-TOH-rah)............Long reed that grows near shore in
Lake Titicaca
Tránsito
(TRAN-see-to)............Traffic police
Tunta
(TOON-tah)................Dehydrated potato
Viscacha
(vees-CAH-chah)........Rodent of the high Andes
Yungas
(YOON-gahs)...............Semi-jungle area located on the rug-
ged eastern slopes of the Andes

To order additional copies of

Taken at Gunpoint

please send $9.95* plus $1.50 for
shipping and handling to:

Roscoe Knight
1100 North Meridian #3
Newberg, OR 97132
(503) 538-4762

*Quantity discounts available.